The
Mindful
Kitchen

The Mindful Kitchen

Vegetarian cooking
to relate to nature

Heather Thomas

Leaping Hare Press

First published in the UK and North America in 2019 by
Ivy Press
An imprint of The Quarto Group
The Old Brewery, 6 Blundell Street
London N7 9BH, United Kingdom
T (0)20 7700 6700
www.QuartoKnows.com

ISBN: 978-1-78240-961-8

This book was conceived, designed, and produced by
Ivy Press
58 West Street, Brighton BN1 2RA, UK

PUBLISHER David Breuer
EDITORIAL DIRECTOR Tom Kitch
ART DIRECTOR James Lawrence
COMMISSIONING EDITOR Monica Perdoni
PROJECT EDITOR Stephanie Evans
DESIGN MANAGER Anna Stevens
DESIGNER Michelle Noel
PHOTOGRAPHER Xavier D. Buendia
EDITORIAL ASSISTANT Niamh Jones

Printed in China

10 9 8 7 6 5 4 3 2 1

Contents

Introduction

Getting Reacquainted with Mother Nature

When I was a child, one of my favorite books was *Brother Eagle, Sister Sky: A Message from Chief Seattle*. It centers on the belief held by the North American indigenous people that the earth does not belong to us; instead, we belong to it. I would lose myself in the dreamlike illustrations that accompanied the wisdom shared by the respected tribal leader, Chief Seattle. He explained: "We did not weave the web of life, we are merely a strand in it. Whatever we do to the web, we do to ourselves." More than a century and a half ago, Seattle was making an impassioned plea that when we harm the earth, we are also harming the people who live on the earth. Today, in a world where experiencing anxiety and depression is normal, in which loneliness has become an epidemic, and where human-induced climate change and environmental degradation have resulted in or are threatening the extinction of many species (including ourselves), there are clearly some loose strands in our web. So, how do we mend it? Can the business of being human support abundance for all forms of life? The good news is that there is scientific, economic, sociological, and psychological evidence that says that we can. So *why don't we?*

Simply put, change can be tough. And the changes required to build a better world for all are complex. In my Mindful Kitchen workshops, almost every week someone says something along the lines of: "Trying to live my values in this world is exhausting. I want to be the change, but I feel like I am constantly making compromises. Then I beat myself up." Completely understandable. However, beating ourselves up is not going to get us anywhere. Movements that make the world a fairer place are generally not built on the foundations of fear, shame, and self-loathing. Instead, they are built on humility, empathy, wonder, compassion, and, the ingredient that connects them all—love.

> "We did not weave the web of life, we are merely a strand in it. Whatever we do to the web, we do to ourselves."

I stay energized by reminding myself that we are living in a world in transition. The changes required to build regenerative systems (economic, energy, food, and transport systems) are much bigger than I am. Collectively, we need to stop fearing and feeding systems that do not serve us or the life on which we depend. Transformation will result from the accumulation of a multitude of seemingly small actions. Yet, we must push the transition toward a more equitable world for all forms of life, without fostering unrealistic expectations that any one of us can behave as if we dwell in that world already. This book offers suggestions on how to create sustainable change using food as the tool that viscerally connects us to all of nature.

Expanding Identity

Impactful behavior change begins with mindset change, encapsulated by the phrase "from head to hands to habit." What type of systems would we create if we all thought of ourselves as interdependent parts of nature? The systems that we designed to run our human-centric world are built on a dualist assumption: the "us" in the equation is people and the "them" is nature. What if we were to reframe that assumption? Instead of valuing our human independence from nature, what if we built systems that recognized the interconnectedness and, going deeper into Chief Seattle's web, the interdependence of all forms of life? These are the types of questions that eco-psychologists who study nature relatedness ask. Nature relatedness is the extension of your identity beyond the human realm (brother/sister, teacher/pupil, athlete/couch potato . . . you get my meaning) to the all-encompassing natural worldwide web. If you hold a nature-related identity, when you go for a walk in the woods, you go beyond admiring its beauty. As you breathe in the scent of flowers, listen to the crunch of fallen leaves beneath your feet, or admire the nobility of the tree that soars above—you feel as secure as you do at home, as though you are a part of the woods.

Researchers have discovered that the more we begin to identify as being a part of nature (which can be measured by plotting your perspectives on a nature-relatedness scale) we decrease our stress and anxiety levels, enhance our cognitive and creative abilities, and, by default, we begin to adopt more ecologically beneficial behaviors. Essentially, identifying AS nature improves our lives and the life upon which we are dependent.

Human identity is malleable but change doesn't happen overnight. Practice leads to progress. If we are eventually to nail a Mozart concerto, we have to start by playing simple scales. Nature relatedness is the same as mastering the piano. Our identity shifts over time if we repeatedly approach experiences in nature with an open-minded intent to create change. Yet, as more than half the human population now lives in urban jungles, nature increasingly feels as though it is out there, something separate from us, hard to access daily. Reform that thought!

There is one thing that we do every day, cannot avoid, and probably enjoy, which reinforces our identity as an interdependent part of the natural world, if we choose to let it—and that is eat. Pause for a moment and consider how every morsel of food that you have ever eaten has been brought to you by a well-nigh magical collaboration of people, plants, animals, wind, water, soil, sun, and countless tiny microorganisms that you will probably never see.

Food is the great connector of life. Each time we put a bite of food into our mouths, we are in a process of exchange with the entire natural world that created and sustains us. The word "exchange" implies reciprocation. And when we exchange gifts, we give as well as receive. What an opportunity for mindset shift!

About this Book

The Mindful Kitchen offers you a blueprint for building a nature-relatedness practice through the food you eat. The aim of this book is to help you develop the skills you need to read the language of nature on your plate, to help you nurture your relationship with yourself as a part of nature and, in doing so, to shift your mindset to foster your ability to play your part in creating a regenerative world that fosters abundance for all forms of life. With due diligence, along the way you should begin to see your behavior shifting in a more ecologically friendly way.

What are more ecologically friendly food behaviors? Eating more local, organically produced plant-based foods (and wasting less of them) on a seasonal basis is the general rule of thumb, supported by the recipes in this book. But also critical is the impact the production of those plant-based foods has on maintaining the ability of the ecosystem to regenerate itself. That means considering the role that some livestock have in maintaining the balance of an ecosystem long since adapted to their presence. For example, evidence shows that livestock are important for keeping soil healthy and maintaining microbiotic diversity that other life-forms, including humans, need for maintaining resistance to disease. That is why I include vegetarian as well as vegan recipes in this book.

The point here is that the food system is complex. To make ecologically balanced choices requires a person to be able to consider complex variables that are difficult to boil down to a "one size fits all" list. *The Mindful Kitchen* aims to equip you with the skills you need to ask the questions to develop your understanding of what a regenerative food system looks like in your local area. A regenerative food system is one in which land—in particular, the soil—is restored as it is used in a system that creates positive loops for all connected natural resources. In regenerative systems, humans aim to learn from mother nature and adopt the role of nurturing caretaker—as opposed to trying to outsmart and dominate her.

Developing that nurturing mindset is a shift for most of us as our contemporary world is mainly built upon the latter philosophy. Making informed choices means being able to analyze a situation based on knowledge. Building a nature-related practice enables you to gradually develop the awareness and the ability to shape the questions that lead to more nuanced answers, ones that consider biodiversity, soil fertility, equitable access to water, land usage, greenhouse gas emissions, food distribution, and what fair food prices mean. This book cannot answer all those questions for you, not least because everyone's situation is different. But, I think more important, I hope this book will help you to shift your mindset toward being a nurturing part of nature and, through that process, equip you with the ability to ask questions that enable you to seek answers, develop your intent to do so, and share the answers. A mindful kitchen is an empowered one.

This book is structured to help you develop your ability to eat and cook with different goals from those you may currently have. Chapter 1, Eating for Vitality, explores how true nourishment is a collaborative act, and how eating for health requires holistic thinking. The second chapter, Eating for Comfort, explores the sensual nature of food and how we can train the sensory receptors in our eyes, nose, and mouth to connect our brains to a world well beyond our plate. Chapter 3, Eating for Creativity, explores how we can look at the foods we eat every day in a new way. Eating for Connection, Chapter 4, explores how eating can become a vehicle through which we deepen our bonds with other humans (past and present) and all forms of life.

The final chapter, Eating for Celebration, explores how feasting began as a way to honor the collective and asks what you want to honor through the food that you eat. Some chapters offer a collection of recipes designed for you to share your nature-relatedness practice with a gathering of those you love, like the feasts of old. Yet, all the recipes are adaptable to be quiet meals for one and frenzied midweek dishes for the whole family that can nonetheless be transformed to nature-related moments.

The Mindful Kitchen offers a "recipe for life," not just a meal. I invite you to lean into a process that blends cooking and mindfulness to develop a nature-related practice. Each chapter also delivers exercises that build the foundations of our practice; Storytelling, Beginner's Mind, and Rituals. Some rituals incorporate the natural world beyond your plate, some appear in the form of recipes. As your identity begins to shift, these foundations begin to blur into a harmonious repertoire. Intent simply becomes your way of being human, by being nature. I like to think Chief Seattle would approve.

Storytelling

The food on your plate has a humbling and awe-inspiring story to tell, if you choose to listen. In every meal lurks a tale of the epic journey of billions of humans who came before you. In every bite lurks the song of the heavens, the earth, and the water that flows. Those lyrics are written in the language of nature and The Mindful Kitchen is here to help you develop your fluency. Learning a new language requires study. I hope to help you to build new knowledge by offering stories about the history of food, anthropology, and ecology. If from time to time you find yourself thinking, I never thought of food that way, then bingo! That is mindset shift in action and soon you will be asking new questions about what you want your story with food to be.

Those are the questions that will help you seek out new knowledge from other sources and apply what I talk about from my perch in Copenhagen, to your part of the world. Knowledge is power.

Beginner's Mind

Einstein once wrote: "To raise new questions, new possibilities, to regard old problems from a new angle requires creative imagination and marks real advance in science." Yes and, Albert, I think cultivating a sense of wonder marks every advance in abundance in every life ever lived. It all begins with nurturing your ability to form questions, and at the same time free yourself from knowing the answer. It feels great! Have you ever watched a child look at a leaf or a spider or a box with obvious delight? In the process of learning, children don't assume they know what they see. They simply take joy in exploration. Imagine how much joy you could find in what you perceive to be the mundanity of everyday if you were to do the same.

Cultivating your Beginner's Mind is your ticket to childlike wonder. It is also your ticket to gradually building your knowledge of the intersection of the natural world and the way we have designed our food system, enabling you not only to make choices that better suit your values, but also to channel forward the creative inspiration for change. You begin to see the world differently. Food is a marvelous place to start. Regularly asking endlessly adaptable questions, such as What part of a plant does this food come from? What value does this food offer to other parts of nature beyond feeding humans?, or What meaning does this food hold for me, beyond being food, and why?, will help you to perceive food as a conduit to the entire natural world. The value of all food in your life, from a full-on celebratory meal to a morning cup of coffee, will grow. As it does, eventually, your behaviors will shift as your world becomes more wondrous.

> "To raise new questions, new possibilities, to regard old problems from a new angle requires creative imagination and marks real advance in science."

Rituals

Beginner's mind questioning enables your mind to develop a better understanding of how your lifestyle reflects your values and brings renewed wonder to your everyday life. But, how do you translate intention into habitual action, particularly if you are trying to bring about change? The answer is a commitment to bringing new awareness and meaning to the rituals we all partake in each day. As symbolic anthropologist Clifford Geertz once remarked, "man is an animal suspended in webs of significance he himself has spun." How do you act out the significance that the all-connecting food web holds? Be it birthday cake, Sunday lunch, or Thanksgiving, food rituals fill us with a sense of security and meaning. The things we do ritualistically are extensions of who we are as people. Quite often in life we inherit rituals without questioning their relevance. Rarely do we set our intent to developing rituals that enable us to create change in our life and the life that surrounds us. Every recipe in this book invites you to infuse the process of creating a meal with intent to be the humble, empathetic, compassionate individual you hope to be in a world that honestly reflects the interdependence of all life.

Heady as that sounds, in reality many of the rituals we partake in already mirror the cycles of nature, because they stem from a time when people saw themselves as a part of nature, not beings who could dominate it. For example, take Halloween,. Its origins go back 2,000 years to the time of the Celts living in Great Britain and northern France. After the autumnal equinox, when misty mornings and long dark nights began to draw in as the fertile world became dormant for months on end, it was bound to be frightening. People put lights in their windows and made offerings of food to the spirits to appease them. Every Halloween, when we have fun carving out faces in candlelit pumpkins to set on our doorsteps and windowsills, or give treats to children dressed as ghosts and ghouls who come knocking, we are reenacting the same cycle of life in connection to nature that our distant ancestors did. Every food ritual presents an opportunity to better understand the language of nature and to weave a web of significance that serves all. *The Mindful Kitchen* helps you to start weaving that web, from head to hands to habit.

How to Select Ingredients

Cooking to enhance your identity as a part of nature leads to your developing greater awareness of the ingredients you choose to eat. The intent is for the recipes in this book to be eaten only seasonally, in accordance with the earth's annual journey around the sun, and made from ingredients produced by regional farms engaged in agroecological practices often sent to market with organic and biodynamic labels. If you can't find exactly what the recipe suggests, get creative and modify, based on what you can find that is local, seasonal, and organic. While that may raise more questions and more habit changes, it will only add to your nature-related experience.

> "Man is an animal suspended in webs of significance he himself has spun."

Eating for Vitality

Cultivating Collaboration
With All of Nature

You are what you eat. Most often, people interpret that phrase as meaning you are as physically healthy as the food you put into your body. Research is emerging that paints a more holistic picture about health and food. Studies indicate that the food we eat also affects our mental and emotional well-being. Food impacts how we see and behave in the world, begging the question: Are we what we eat?

Every one of us has an individual responsibility for our own vitality, yet nourishment is a collaborative act that extends far beyond human life. Every time we sit down to a meal, we are reminded of our dependence upon the earth. Food is vital for all of life, not just humans, and our vitality is interlinked.

Striving to eat primarily local, seasonal, plant-based, organic foods (and to waste far less of them by using, not discarding, the peels, skins, and seeds, and by preserving foods to extend their season), is about resilience and regeneration for us and the life on which we depend in a climate that is rapidly changing. Redeveloping our food system calls on all of us to be our most collaborative and creative selves. Eating for collective vitality as a nature-related practice nurtures the mental and emotional well-being we derive from heightening our identity as a part of our environment, which in turn begins to shift our habits toward more eco-friendly behavior.

By eating more locally produced food, your ties are strengthened to the place where you live, beyond what you see on your plate. As your awareness grows, it becomes difficult not to connect weather patterns and animal and insect life to the foods available in your market. Through eating, you become more oriented toward the life around you.

If what is on our plates changes with the seasons of our local communities, we strengthen this effect as we let our bodies and minds shift in

tune with life around us. The more we tap into the importance of all elements of our ecosystem, the more we begin to understand the value of biodiversity. Our expectation that we can have whatever food we want to have at our fingertips year-round has a huge impact on biodiversity loss. Intensively produced monocrops (for example, avocados or bananas) require deforestation in the name of dedicating land to the production of one species at the expense of most others. Considering the interdependence of life in an ecosystem, this inherently limits long-term resilience.

The United Nations Food and Agricultural Organization (FAO) reports that genetically uniform monocrop practices have led to a 75 percent loss of plant genetic diversity worldwide. Today, 75 percent of our food is generated from 12 crops and five animal species. Opening our eyes to what surrounds us, in the way our ancient ancestors explored what is edible, and expanding our palate to support local biodiversity stimulates wonder and creativity, and it serves us regeneratively.

The Invisible Life upon
Which Your Vitality Depends

A single tablespoon of fertile soil can hold more life forms than there are humans on the earth. The overwhelming majority of our diet grows in soil. Many people aim to eat more organic and biodynamic food, wanting to digest fewer chemicals. The fewer chemicals we pour on the soil, the healthier all the life in this ecosystem will be, too. Soil is a finite resource, meaning it takes longer than a human lifetime to regenerate degraded soil. Considering that the UN FAO reports that more than 30 percent of the world's fertile soil has been degraded and that caring for it through regenerative farming techniques (which also promote biodiversity) can increase overall yields of food for humans, prioritizing eating organic and biodynamic food is a choice that fosters holistic vitality.

Learning New Habits

Anyone who has tried to lose weight knows that changing how you eat is no easy task. Our eating habits are deeply embedded in our routines, fueled by cultural meaning and lifestyle. Wanting to make change is step one. Translating desire into action takes a plan, patience, and compassion. Change requires reflection on what motivates your behavior, changing your motivation story as you set new intent, building new knowledge to reinforce your new story, and ritualistically taking part in new activities so that you can translate your thoughts into new habits that stay with you. You won't shed pounds overnight, and you won't begin to feel the benefits of a nature-related practice overnight. Repeat practice is what leads to progress.

The first step in building a nature-relatedness practice with food is learning how to eat for vitality. Eating for vitality starts by reconsidering the holistic nature of nourishment. Making "healthy" food choices that harm the environment on which all life depends does not serve vitality. Approaching meals as an opportunity to deepen your understanding of how your vitality depends on life beyond the human realm is the starting point for your nature-related practice with food.

Ritual

Eating for Vitality: The Food Web

Pause briefly to consider a triangle versus a circle. Traditional food chain thinking lends itself to the triangle shape.

Humans sit at the pinnacle of a hierarchy of life-forms. If we place a pizza in this context, a hungry person is at the top of the pyramid, below which are: the person who runs the local pizzeria; the cows that produced milk for the cheese; the grass the cows grazed, the bees that pollinated the tomatoes, the ladybugs that ate the aphids, the soil in which the wheat grew, and so on. Food chain thinking is limited to the human point of view. At its best, the humans on top aim to be benevolent masters of other life-forms.

In biology, food chains are part of a bigger story, food webs. These contain several interconnected food chains. To reconsider our pizza in the context of a food web,

picture a circle. There is no hierarchy. Hungry people, working people, cows, plants, grass, insects, soil, and the wood fueling the oven each plays an equal part in pizza creation. When we start to think from the perspective of the web, we begin to consider what is healthy for us, for the whole, and vice versa.

Next time you sit down to eat, approach the food on your plate in the context of the food chain, then in the context of the food web. Think triangle, then think circle. Do you ask different questions? The more you consider how the health of other life-forms impacts your own, the more your nature-relatedness practice is building and the more you will find yourself eating for collective vitality.

The recipes in this chapter are intended to be eaten in early fall, because my inspiration came from the Jewish holiday Sukkot, which celebrates the gathering of the harvest. Practicing Jews eat their meals outdoors in a tabernacle to honor a time when their ancestors were protected when traveling in the desert. The guidelines for building the tabernacle include leaving gaps in the roof to see the stars and feel the wind and rain. A perfect environment to raise a toast to *L'chaim*: To life— to vitality for all.

Flatbread

Makes

4

Ingredients

2½ cups all-purpose flour, plus extra for dusting

½ teaspoon salt

¼ cup olive oil

¾ cup oat milk

½–1 tablespoon vegetable oil, for cooking

How can the way you eat make you feel more connected to the rest of the natural world?

I offer you this simple flatbread recipe with the hope that you will use your hands to eat many of these dishes and consider how doing so speaks to something deep inside you.

Archaeobotanists have discovered that flatbread is a staple of human vitality that predates the agricultural revolution. As early as 14,400 years ago, nomadic hunter-gatherers were making flatbread. Imagine foraging for wild cereals, dehusking them, grinding them with stones, mixing them with water, kneading dough, and baking it on hot stones over an open fire. Without romanticizing the labor, I like to consider how connected to the full cycle of nature those humans must have felt preparing and eating this simple flatbread.

Method

1. Combine the flour, salt, oil, and oat milk in a bowl to make a soft dough. Sprinkle the work surface with flour, turn out the dough, and knead for a few minutes until it is smooth. Add another teaspoon or two of flour if it is too sticky.

2. Wrap the dough in a dish towel and let it rest in the refrigerator for about 30 minutes.

3. Dust the work surface with flour again. Cut your dough into four even pieces, roll into balls, then roll out into thin rounds (about ¼ inch thick).

4. Spread the oil evenly across a nonstick skillet and put it over medium heat. Place one flatbread in the pan. It will puff up on one side; when it does, flip it and cook the other side. If it puffs up too much, pat it gently to break the air bubble. You are looking for golden brown spots on both sides. Keep flipping until you are happy. Use your fingers as well as a spatula for the process. It should take about 2 minutes to cook each flatbread.

5. Stack the cooked bread on a plate as you make the rest and keep a dish towel on hand to cover the bread and trap in the heat.

Tip You can make flatbread in advance and freeze them. Make sure they are completely cool and pat them with paper towels to be sure the surface is dry. Stack them in a freezerproof container, layered with parchment paper, and put them into the freezer. When you want to use some, remove them from the freezer to thaw. Preheat the oven to 300°F, then add a drop or two of water to each flatbread and put into the oven for about 10 minutes to warm.

Labneh

Cheese was discovered, not invented. Legend has it that an Arab traveler packed milk for a long, hot journey and discovered that as the milk jostled, it was transformed. Instead of drinking milk, he dined on a rudimentary cottage cheese, a salty liquid and perhaps, many questions. As you make this labneh, pause to marvel at the complexity of collaboration of the different forms of life required to make foods that we deem to be simple.

Serves
6

Ingredients
1½ cups Greek-style yogurt
½ teaspoon lemon juice
¼ cup olive oil
2 tablespoons zaatar or paprika
Pinch of sea salt

Equipment
12-inch square piece of cheesecloth
Kitchen string

Method
1. Mix together the yogurt, lemon juice, and salt.

2. Lay a piece of cheesecloth on top of a bowl. Now place your yogurt mixture in the middle of the cloth. Pull the sides together and tie with a length of string. Gently squeeze the little cheese ball to form an egglike shape.

3. Hang the bundle in your refrigerator. I use a piece of tape and a pickle jar to hold it in place. Place a bowl underneath your bundle to catch the dripping whey. Let stand for 24 hours.

4. Remove from the refrigerator, unwrap your labneh, and put it onto a serving plate. Drizzle with olive oil, sprinkle with zaatar or paprika to add some color, and serve.

> **How is inventing a food different from discovering a food?**
> The tale of the Arab traveler is a reminder of the invisible life that surrounds us and with which we are in constant exchange.

Tzatziki

Tzatziki shines when it is served as the cool sidekick to feistier characters. The good life isn't just about the shouting from the rooftop moments, it's about balancing the big stuff with joy found in everyday moments. That's tzatziki, the cream to complement the extremes. And, on a practical note, you can make it if you find you have leftover Greek yogurt from making labneh.

Serves
4

Ingredients

½ cucumber, washed and scrubbed

1 cup Greek-style yogurt (or use nondairy yogurt, if you prefer)

1 tablespoon olive oil

1 garlic clove, finely chopped

A handful each of fresh dill and mint leaves, plus extra for serving

Juice of ½ lemon

Zest of 1 preserved lemon (page 38; optional)

Pinch of salt

Method

1. Cut the cucumber in half lengthwise, then use a spoon to scoop out the seeds. Chop the flesh into small dice, as you would dice an onion. Roll the dice in a dish towel and gently press to remove excess moisture before adding to a bowl.

2. Mix in the yogurt, then add the oil and garlic and mix. Finely chop the dill and mint. Add it to the mix with your lemon juice and preserved lemon zest (optional) and give it one last stir.

3. Transfer to a serving bowl and decorate with herbs before serving alongside something spicy, such as shakshuka (page 33).

> **How did the foods you eat most often become thought of as food?**
> The mysteries of how our foods were discovered and cultivated impacts your everyday vitality.

Fava Bean Falafel

Fava beans have been part of our diet for at least 6,000 years. I use them to make falafel, another staple dish of the Middle East and a common street food. These are delicious wrapped in flatbread and served with salad and tahini.

Serves
2 as a main or 4 as a side

Ingredients
1½ cups whole dried fava beans

2 tablespoons baking soda, plus an extra ½ teaspoon

Handful each of parsley and cilantro, leaves and stems

1 small onion, finely chopped

2 garlic cloves

1½ teaspoons all-purpose flour

1 teaspoon ground cumin

½ teaspoon chili powder

1 teaspoon salt

Juice of 1 lemon

Canola oil, for frying

Method

1. Put the dried beans with 2 tablespoons of baking soda into cold water to soak for 24 hours. Halfway through the soaking time, peel off their skins and split the beans.

2. Drain and rinse the beans. Pulse the herbs, onion, garlic, the ½ teaspoon of baking soda, flour, cumin, chili powder, salt, and half the lemon juice in a food processor until it has a pesto-like consistency. Add the beans and the remaining lemon juice and process until the mixture becomes a coarse paste.

3. Let the mixture rest for 30 minutes to let the flavor settle. Shape into golf ball-size falafels.

4. Put a large skillet onto the stove and pour in enough canola oil to cover the falafels (about 1 inch deep). Warm the oil over high heat until bubbles form around a wooden spoon inserted into the oil. Add the falafels (you may need to work in batches) and fry them for 4–5 minutes, until crisp and cooked through, turning to brown on all sides.

5. Scoop out the falafels with a slotted spoon and place on a plate lined with an old dish towel to absorb the excess oil. Serve warm with tabbouleh on the side, some tahini or hummus for dipping, and flatbread.

Tip There's no need to discard the oil. Let it cool, strain off any pieces of falafel, and pour into a bottle for the next time you make falafels. The same oil can be used up to four times.

What aspects of food remind you of the rest of the natural world?
The burst of green inside the brown crust of a falafel reminds me how eating is an act that connects us to an entire ecosystem, something our early ancestors probably understood better than we do today.

Tahini

Growing in drought-prone regions of the world we think of as the cradle of civilization, the resilient sesame is intent on spreading life. Its ripening seeds swell in the pod until eventually it bursts. Open sesame: Food is shared and more sesame is produced. Fittingly, just as sesame was a building block of cultivation and the world of food as we know it, tahini is the basis of many recipes here—a reminder that our vitality is interwoven with life that has gone before.

Makes
About ⅔ cup

Ingredients
1 cup sesame seeds
3–5 tablespoons canola oil or olive oil
Pinch of salt

Method

1. Add the sesame seeds to a dry skillet over medium heat, tossing until they begin to release their aroma. Hulled seeds have had their coats removed, unhulled are darker in color, a little more bitter tasting, and produce a slightly coarser paste. Experiment to learn which you prefer.

2. Transfer the toasted seeds to a baking sheet to cool. Place them in a food processor and process for 1 minute to produce a crumbly paste. Add 3 tablespoons of olive oil and a pinch of salt. Process for another 3 minutes. Add more oil and process again for a more liquid tahini.

3. Use your tahini as a stand-alone dip, pour it on roasted veg, or use it as an ingredient in the recipes that follow. It keeps in a jar in the refrigerator for about a month. If it separates, just stir it.

> **How are the foods you eat today tied to human history?**
> Sesame is one of the oldest cultivated plants, and one of the first that could provide us not just with an oil to sustain our bodies, but one to be burned for light, providing us comfort in the darkness.

Smoky Baba ghanoush

When the eggplant first made its way, via Sicily, to mainland Italy, people were suspicious of this new gleaming, purple-skinned vegetable and named it *mela insana*, "apple of insanity," thinking anyone daring enough to eat it would surely go mad. Fortunately, the eggplant (*melanzana* in Italian) proved its worth and is now an essential ingredient in several Sicilian signature dishes.

Makes
About ⅔ cup

Ingredients
2 eggplants

1 teaspoon paprika, preferably smoked

1 teaspoon ground cumin

2 tablespoons olive oil

2 garlic cloves

1 heaping teaspoon zaatar (optional)

1 tablespoon tahini, preferably homemade (page 25)

Juice of 2 lemons

Pinch of salt

Method
1. Preheat the broiler to medium.

2. Cut the eggplants in half lengthwise and score the surface, making crisscross cuts about one-third of the way through the flesh. Place them cut side up on a small baking sheet.

3. Mix together the paprika, cumin, and olive oil. Brush the mixture over the eggplants (or use the back of a spoon). Put the baking sheet under the broiler until the eggplants are soft and the juices start to run. Watch carefully: Don't let the tops become too brown—you want the flesh to be gooey inside—so cover if need be.

4. Remove the eggplants and set aside to cool for 15 minutes. Scoop the eggplant flesh from the skins and put it into the food processor along with the garlic, zaatar, and tahini, and process. Add the lemon juice, a pinch or two of salt, and process again. Check and adjust the flavor and consistency to your preference.

> **When did the foods you think of as your national cuisine become a part of your cultural traditions?**
> Food culture is dynamic and the impact of social change can often be observed on our plates.

Hummus

I like to picture our ancestors making this same dish alfresco, using a mortar and pestle to pound their chickpeas to a paste. Even using a food processor, the principle is exactly the same. I tend to make my hummus a little on the dry side, with less fat. That means, instead of using all of the tahini to make this recipe, I have some left over to drizzle on roasted vegetables.

Serves
6

Ingredients
2 cups dried chickpeas
1 vegetable bouillon cube
2 bay leaves
Pinch of baking soda
5 garlic cloves
⅔ cup tahini (page 25)
Juice of 2 lemons
5–6 tablespoons olive oil
Pinch of salt
Zaatar or paprika, to serve

Method
1. Put the chickpeas into a bowl, cover with cold water, and rehydrate for 24 hours. Rehydrated beans look smaller than canned ones, which sit in liquid for months so they are bloated— I find them less flavorful than rehydrated ones.

2. Drain and rinse your chickpeas. Transfer them to a large saucepan with the bouillon cube, bay leaves, baking soda, and garlic. Add enough water to cover the chickpeas, bring to a boil, and let them simmer for 40 minutes. Using a slotted spoon, skim off any skins that have risen to the surface. Drain the chickpeas, discarding the bay leaves and garlic. Let cool, then remove the skins from the chickpeas and put them into a food processor. Add the tahini, lemon juice, 4 tablespoons of olive oil and 2 tablespoons of cold water. Process. Check the consistency and taste: Is it what YOU like? If yes, then voilà! If not, add more oil and/or a tablespoon of cold water until you have the consistency and flavor you prefer.

3. To serve, swirl a heaping tablespoonful onto a small plate, drizzle with olive oil, and dust with zaatar or paprika.

How does the process of making hummus make you feel?

When making food becomes as much about the process as the end product, it can become a means to internalize how you, too, are a part of nature.

Variation: Roasted Carrot Hummus

Variety is the spice of life! Creatively adapt this recipe using what is to be found in your refrigerator or pantry.

Method
1. Follow the recipe for hummus and, while the chickpeas are simmering, preheat the oven to 400°F.

2. Scrub, peel, and slice 6 carrots into sticks. Transfer to a roasting pan. Mix 1 tablespoon ground cumin with 2 tablespoons olive oil and pour over the carrots. Roast for 20 minutes, or until soft. Remove and cool.

3. Continue with the recipe, adding the cooled carrots to the processed hummus and process again to combine. Check the consistency as before.

Variation: Lima Bean and Rosemary Hummus

Cooking to promote biodiversity means trying alternatives, such as lima beans instead of chickpeas, in your hummus.

Method
1. Follow the recipe for hummus but use 2 cups of dried lima beans in place of chickpeas. While your beans are simmering, preheat the oven to 425°F. Slice a head of garlic to expose the cloves. Drizzle 1 teaspoon of olive oil on the garlic and roast in the oven for 30–40 minutes, until the flesh is completely soft.

2. Continue with the recipe, adding the garlic and 2 tablespoons of dried rosemary to the food processor before processing. Check the consistency as before.

3. Sprinkle with dried rosemary in place of the paprika or zaatar.

Tabbouleh

Herbs are underappreciated. What would eating experiences be without their subtle flavor and cheerful splash of color? Tabbouleh is all about the herbs. In the Levant, this simple dish is traditionally served as part of a mezze, its fresh flavors sharpened with lemon juice. You can achieve the same acid zing using a locally produced apple cider vinegar.

Serves
6

Ingredients
⅔ cup bulgur wheat
½ vegetable bouillon cube
4 tomatoes
1 cucumber
1 red onion
3 handfuls of parsley leaves
1 handful of mint leaves
3–6 tablespoons apple cider vinegar
¼ cup olive oil
Salt

Method
1. Rinse the bulgur wheat, then cover in boiling water, adding the half bouillon cube for extra flavor. Let stand for 15 minutes, then drain and put the bulgur into the refrigerator to cool.

2. Chop all the vegetables into small pieces. Don't bother peeling the cucumber, because the peels hold in the water and keep your salad fresher. Along the same lines, drain the excess juice from your tomatoes.

3. Put the chopped vegetables, herbs, and chilled bulgur into a serving bowl. Add the vinegar, tasting as you do so, the olive oil, and salt and mix. Keep in the refrigerator until ready to serve—the crisper the salad the more the herb flavors zing.

Which parts of nature are involved in developing the foods you eat most often?
Tabbouleh is essentially a parsley and mint salad, and preparing and eating it reminds me how easy it is to overlook all the life that surrounds me and makes my life worth living.

Maple-drizzled Roast Butternut Squash

For me, fall is not complete without eating squash, which includes melons, cucumbers, and gourds. Squash were eaten by camels and horses that spread seeds as they roamed. Eventually, humans in Central America began to cultivate squash. As summer transitions into fall, butternut squash, brought to you by the collaboration of many forms of life, deserves a place at the table.

Serves

6

Ingredients

1–2 tablespoons olive oil

1 medium butternut squash, scrubbed clean

1 red onion, halved, then cut lengthwise into long thin strips

3 garlic cloves, minced

1 tablespoon minced fresh ginger

Handful of pitted, chopped dates

2 tablespoons zaatar

1 tablespoon maple syrup (or honey)

Salt and pepper

Parsley or cilantro sprigs, to garnish

Method

1. Preheat the oven to 400°F and oil a large baking sheet.

2. Cut the butternut squash at the bottom of its "neck" (because this is a slow-roasted squash, there is no need to peel it). Use a spoon to scoop the seeds and fibers from the "bowl" of the squash. Now chop your flesh into medium-size chunks.

3. Transfer the squash and onion to the baking sheet, drizzle with a tablespoon of oil, and season with salt and pepper. Stir to coat. Evenly space the vegetables and roast for 20 minutes, stirring occasionally. Add the garlic, ginger, dates, and zaatar and roast for another 10 minutes. Remove from the oven and pile into a serving bowl. Drizzle the maple syrup over the top and garnish with parsley or cilantro before serving.

> **How do animals that you do not eat play a role in your food system?**
> When you lean into food-web thinking, you discover that animals you might not eat are critical, because they balance populations that support biodiverse harmony.

Shakshuka with Sweet Potatoes and Brussels Sprouts

Many cultures observe periods of abstinence from eating to instill gratitude for abundance that is easily taken for granted. We all have a small fast period while we sleep at night. Breakfast is a daily moment to consider the value of food and the life on which we are interdependent. Shakshuka is traditionally a breakfast food. Serve it family style and celebrate nourishment made collaboratively, served communally. Any leftover filling makes a delicious lunch.

Serves
4

Ingredients

1 tablespoon olive oil

1 teaspoon ground cumin

1 teaspoon ground paprika

¼ teaspoon ground cinnamon

1 large red onion, thinly sliced

2 tablespoons ginger juice (or use ginger beer)

4 medium sweet potatoes (about 1½ pounds), peeled and cubed

1 pound Brussels sprouts, trimmed and quartered if large

¼ cup broth made with ½ vegetable bouillon cube

1 (14½-ounce) can of diced tomatoes

4 eggs

Salt and pepper

Torn cilantro or parsley leaves, to serve

Method

1. Preheat the oven to 400°F.

2. Heat the oil in an 11–12 inch ovenproof skillet over medium-low heat. Add the cumin, paprika, and cinnamon. Let the spices sizzle in the oil for 30 seconds before adding the sliced onion and ginger juice and cook down for about 8 minutes, until the onion has softened.

3. Add the sweet potatoes, sprouts, broth, and tomatoes. Cover the pan with a lid and cook over medium–low heat for 30–40 minutes, until the vegetables are soft, stirring occasionally.

4. Using the back of a spoon, make a well in the tomato mixture, crack an egg, and pour it into the well. Repeat with the other eggs. You may want to add a pinch of salt to each one.

5. Transfer the skillet to the oven and bake for 7–10 minutes, depending on how firm you like your yolks. When the eggs are baked, add a dash of pepper and some herbs. Bring the skillet to the table and serve hot.

> **How can food rituals, such as abstaining from eating for a time, help you better understand your role in the food system?**
>
> Abstinence often helps you to build gratitude for things you take for granted or simply don't notice.

Orange-roasted Cauliflower with Dates

Mark Twain wrote in his 1894 novel *Pudd'nhead Wilson*: "Training is everything. The peach was once a bitter almond; cauliflower is nothing but cabbage with a college education." Oh, to live in a time when vegetables were so valued that Twain chose to use them as an analogy for the human condition! Here is a roasted cauliflower dish, inspired by Twain, with which to play with vitality.

Serves
4

Ingredients

1 cauliflower, cut into individual florets

½ red onion, cut lengthwise into long thin slices

5 tablespoons olive oil

2 tablespoons ginger juice (or use orange juice)

1 orange, peeled and sectioned

½ teaspoon ground cumin

½ teaspoon ground cardamom

½ cup pitted dates

Salt and pepper

Method

1. Preheat the oven to 400°F.

2. Put the cauliflower and onion into a baking dish and mix with the oil, ginger juice, orange, and spices. Roast for 10 minutes. Remove from the oven, add the dates, and cook for another 5 minutes. Remove from the oven, stir to coat, transfer to a serving dish and season with salt and pepper before serving.

> **How can changing the stories you tell yourself about food also change your sense of connection to the rest of the natural world?**
>
> When you tell the story of food from the perspective of the cauliflower, as opposed to the hungry person, it can shift your mindset.

Ritual

Preserved Lemons

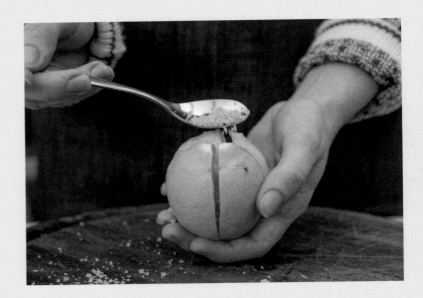

Makes

When making these with a group, I use small screw-top jars and allow for 2 lemons per person

Ingredients

Salt (I use a kosher or large-grain sea salt)
Lemons

Before the food system became industrialized, communities would gather together to preserve food. To carry on this communal tradition, throughout the harvest season, I like to make preserves with friends, sometimes as a game at a dinner party. Preserved lemons, a food staple in the cradle of civilization, are simple to make and represent a way for you to share your nature-relatedness practice with others—a particularly apt thing to do when eating for collective vitality!

Method

1. Preheat the oven to 275°F. Sterilize the jars and their lids using the method on page 60.

2. Cover the bottom of your jar with a thin layer of salt. Cut your lemon in quarters, either cutting right through or leaving them attached at the bottom. Put a generous pinch of salt on the flesh of each one. Take your first lemon and mush the cut and salted flesh side into the bottom of the jar. You want its juices to run; the lemon juice and salt make the salt solution that will preserve the rinds. Pile the remaining lemon quarters tightly on top of one another. The juices of all the lemons should cover the last piece you insert. If not, dissolve a tablespoon of salt in 1 cup of water and pour enough into the jar to cover.

3. Seal tightly and put the jars into a cool dark place for a month before using. Turn your jar upside down periodically so the salt doesn't settle in the bottom. Once opened, store in the refrigerator, where they will last for six months.

4. To use: Take your whole or a quarter lemon and rinse it under cold water to remove the salty liquid (sometimes called brine). Scrape out the flesh, discarding any seeds, and chop the peel. I like to add the flesh to Middle Eastern tagines and stews.

As you make your preserved lemons, throw out a few beginner's mind questions to your gathering. In this way, beginner's mind and rituals blend and when you make the recipes that follow with your preserves, you will reconnect to your new story about eating for collective vitality: Why do trees create fruit? Are they intended to feed pollinators and soil? Trees cannot move or communicate through speech, so need other survival strategies. Or, why did humans start eating tart and tangy lemons in the first place? Did it serve a purpose? Have our taste buds evolved?

Preserved Lemon Spaghetti

This simple dish makes a bold statement. It is impossible to bring a forkful of pasta drizzled in preserved vitality to your lips and not feel a zest for life. This takes moments to make; once mastered, you have a meal in 20 minutes or less. It is a great go-to for a night when you need a pick-me-up, particularly if you're feeling somewhat run down by the urban jungle, because it tastes like eating sunshine.

Serves
4

Ingredients

1 pound spaghetti
(I prefer whole wheat)

1 tablespoon olive oil

1 onion, sliced

2 garlic cloves, chopped

4 handfuls of fresh spinach
(reserve a few leaves as garnish)

1 handful of walnuts

2 preserved lemon quarters
(page 38), thinly sliced

Salt and pepper

For the sauce

Juice of 4 lemons
(you need ½ cup)

½ cup olive oil

1 teaspoon Dijon mustard

½ cup grated vegetarian hard cheese

Method

1. Bring a large saucepan of salted water to a boil. Add the spaghetti and cook following the package directions.

2. Meanwhile, pour the olive oil into a large skillet and warm over low heat. Add the onion and garlic and cook until translucent.

3. For the sauce, mix the lemon juice, olive oil, Dijon mustard, and cheese in a separate bowl.

4. Add the spinach to the onions and garlic and cook until it softens. Add the walnuts just to warm, stirring so they don't burn.

5. Drain the spaghetti, return it to the pan, and mix in the walnuts, spinach, onions, and garlic. Pour over the lemon sauce, add the preserved lemon, season to taste, and mix once again.

How did your environment feel the day you made your preserves?

Take a mental picture of your surroundings on the day you make your preserves, using all your senses, and see whether the smell of your preserves triggers memories of how you felt.

Oven-baked Preserved Lemon Potatoes

What I like most about cooking with preserved lemons is how the punch they add to simple dishes is the kick that reminds me of the extraordinary nature of our everyday foods. Take the potato. There are more than 4,000 varieties of potatoes, all containing more potassium than a banana and plenty of vitamins C and B. Potatoes nourish your body and soul—if you let them.

Serves
4

Ingredients
4 medium potatoes, thinly sliced
1 medium onion, chopped
2 tablespoons olive oil
1 heaping tablespoon zaatar
Peel from 3 preserved lemon quarters (page 38), chopped
Pinch of salt

Method
1. Preheat the oven to 400°F.

2. Put the potatoes and onion onto a baking sheet and toss with the oil, zaatar, and salt.

3. Roast for 15 minutes, then toss the vegetables and return to the oven for 10 minutes to make sure all sides are roasted.

4. Remove from the oven, add the lemon peel, and season before serving.

> **Which everyday foods would you like to know better?**
> Eating for vitality means considering how the food web helps to produce all the foods we eat. As your perspective shifts, you may find yourself making different food choices.

Pucker-up Preserved Lemon Salad

This is a simple dressing that adds some citrusy summer delight to every winter salad. I like to add a little warmth to my salads, particularly in winter. So, this recipe mixes both warm and cold veg. If you are serving the salad on its own, add an egg or a couple of slices of cheese to make a satisfying meal.

Serves

2 as a main, 4 as a side

Ingredients

2 heads romaine lettuce, chopped

1 tablespoon olive oil

½ onion, chopped

2 portobello mushrooms, wiped, peeled, and sliced

Pinch of chili powder or flakes

Handful of roasted pumpkin seeds (page 160)

For the dressing

8 teaspoons apple cider vinegar

4 teaspoons extra virgin olive oil

1 teaspoon Dijon mustard

2 garlic cloves, minced

Peel from 3 preserved lemon quarters (page 38), thinly sliced

2 teaspoons dried basil

Salt

Method

1. Start by making the dressing. Put the vinegar, oil, and mustard into a bowl and whisk. Stir in the garlic, lemon peel, basil, and a pinch of salt. I let the dressing stand for up to 30 minutes before serving to let the flavors develop.

2. Meanwhile, put the lettuce in a salad bowl. Heat the oil in a pan and sauté the onions until they are translucent before adding the mushrooms and chili powder or flakes. Cook for about 4 minutes, flipping the mushrooms to brown on both sides. Add the warm vegetables to your salad bowl, add the pumpkin seeds and the dressing, and toss before serving.

> **What role do lemons play in nature beyond feeding humans?**
>
> Using your preserved lemon provides an opportunity to flex your food-web thinking muscles, our Eating for Vitality ritual (page 19).

Apple Cake Lasagne

If you had a tasty snack and decide to plant a seed from your apple in the yard, be warned: If it grows into a tree, it will produce an altogether different-tasting apple. In order to plant an orchard of Empire, Fuji, or Pippin, a branch of one of those trees must be grafted onto another to produce similar fruit. Thousands of apple varieties that we humans like to eat (and many more that we don't) grow in Asia, Africa, Europe, Oceania, and the Americas, resulting from millennia of layers of human and natural history. Something to consider as you layer this apple cake lasagne.

Serves
8–10

Ingredients
6 small apples
1½ teaspoons cinnamon
¼ cup sugar

For the cake

1⅓ cups canola oil, plus extra for greasing
2 cups all-purpose flour, plus extra for dusting
½ teaspoon salt
2 teaspoons baking powder
¼ teaspoon baking soda
2 cups sugar
1 tablespoon pure vanilla extract
3 extra-large eggs
¼ cup oat milk

Method

1. Preheat the oven to 350°F and grease a 13 x 9 x 2 inch cake pan with a little oil, then dust with flour.

2. Peel, core, and slice the apples, thinly but not too fine. Save the peel to make apple powder (see page 156 and follow the method). Mix the apples with the cinnamon and sugar and set them aside so that the sugar draws out some of the juice from the apples.

3. Combine the flour, salt, baking powder, baking soda, and sugar in a large bowl. I usually opt for unbleached, local, and organic "white" flour, which in practice is more like whole wheat. This makes the cake more wholesome and denser.

4. Beat together the canola oil, vanilla, eggs, and milk in a separate bowl. Slowly combine the dry and wet ingredients and beat together until there are as few lumps as possible.

5. Pour half the batter into the cake pan, then layer it with half the apple slices. Spread the remaining batter on top, then layer with the rest of your apple slices. Pour any juices from your apples over your cake. Transfer the pan to the oven and bake for about 45 minutes. Check your cake after 45 minutes and return it to the oven at 5-minute intervals until a toothpick inserted in the center comes out clean.

6. Cut into squares and serve. Any leftovers are just as good—if not better—the following day.

A quote most often attributed to Martin Luther reads:

"Even if I knew that tomorrow the world would go to pieces, I would still plant my apple tree."

Elements of nature we see as food often nourish humans physically and emotionally, such as Luther equating apples to hope. People use apples to symbolize eternal life, health, intelligence, and temptation. Unraveling why we find so much meaning in food often reveals the strength of our connection to the rest of the natural world both physically and emotionally.

Consider phrases or symbols of the apple with which you are familiar. Why do you think the apple took on such significance? Where does the story of the relationship of humans and apples begin, and where will it end?

Eating
for
Comfort

Cultivating Nourishment

Is there one comfort food that you gravitate toward to refill your resilience tank? Ever wondered how a grilled cheese sandwich possesses superpowers? Much of that power lies not in the sandwich itself, but, instead, in the way your mind perceives that sandwich.

When the double-fudge chunk calls, I am usually in pursuit of something far more nourishing than pleasure; it's the taste of love I am craving. Research indicates that preferred comfort foods are often those served to us by loved ones from our childhood. The mere smell of peanut butter transports me to quiet wintry mornings with my Dad serving me toasted raisin bread with a generous dollop of peanut butter oozing into the nooks and crannies. To this day, peanut butter is a part of my morning ritual. I have not found a better way to set my daily intent to embody love.

Can the task of changing how we eat to nourish ourselves as an interdependent part of nature be made easier by programming ourselves to feel the soulfulness of comfort food when we munch foods produced in ways that foster a regenerative world? I think so.

Our sense of smell acts as a scout for our brain to trigger emotions, memories, and motivation. It has been shown that scent-evoked nostalgia predicts higher levels of self-esteem, optimism, social connectedness, and meaning in life. What an opportunity to pepper your pleasure with purpose. Ask some beginner's mind questions before you eat and consider how the production of your food impacts on biodiversity, soil fertility, or carbon-absorbing forest cover. Give gratitude if the answers align with your values and make a memory of that emotional nourishment by deeply breathing in the aroma of your food. Repeat the process the next time that same meal is served, and it will gradually

become a part of your nature-related practice, creating an attitude for life that extends way beyond your diet.

For all foods to be comfort foods, slow down and focus not just on your food, but on your wider environment as you eat. Your mood will affect how you perceive your food. This was demonstrated by a research project that compared how people experienced the taste of sorbet after a sports game. Supporters of the winning team found the sorbet to be sweet, whereas the losing fans found it tasted sour. Program the feel-good associations of plugging into nature through eating by looking out your window, considering the feel of air on your skin, breathing deeply, and reminding yourself that eating for comfort has as much to do with what is outside as it has with what's in you.

Ritual

Eating for Comfort: For the Love of Food

Take a moment to reflect on a food that you consider to be a comfort food. What memories does that comfort food trigger? And what kind of feelings does that comfort food trigger? Why do you think it became one of your comfort foods?

Now consider the food web from the Eating for Vitality Ritual (page 19), the triangle (human in charge) world view versus the circle (nature in charge) world view. Tell a story about your food from both perspectives. Does it bring up questions you haven't previously considered? Don't worry about not having the answers, the first step is learning to ask the questions, then you can do some research to discover if the food is produced in a way to provide collective nourishment for people and planet. Once you have had a chance to explore, does this food provide you with more or less comfort? Why or why not?

Eating for Comfort:
For the Big-time Sensuality
of Nature

Gather some aromatic spices and herbs (smells that bring you pleasure) and head to a place that you find comforting. One at a time, bring them to your nose and breathe deeply. Does the smell conjure up memories? Are the memories associated with food? A person? A place? A time in your life? A ritual of importance? Does the scent trigger a connection to memories of any sights or sounds of nature? Now pause and consider your own body in the present moment. How do you feel emotionally? How do you feel physically? Do you feel any sensations relating to the wind, sun, soil, water, animals, plants, or people around you? The next time you eat a meal brought to life by the flavor of the spices and herbs you choose, pause and consider if you can remember the moment you just spent in reflection. What memories and associations return to you? How do they make you feel? Repeating this exercise will help you to tune into a much wider world with every bite and to build an eco-friendly attitude that transcends to new habits that stick.

Cooking for Comfort

When, in the words of one song, the "fish are jumping and the cotton is high," plugging into the sensations of life that surround you is a breeze. This collection of rituals in the form of recipes is designed to pepper your summertime eating with sensual memory-making power. Some of the recipes are for eating in the moment, others are preserves to help you evoke summer comforts in the depths of winter. Making now to eat much later also exercises your long-term thinking—a critical skill for developing an interdependent food-web world view. An afternoon of making preserves can help you become the change, from head to hands to habit. What is more comforting than that?

Green Pea Guacamole

Guac tastes great, but it doesn't bring me comfort when I consider its impact on forests, soil, water, and the web of biodiverse life (people included) that suffers because of a craze for avocados. So when a craving for guacamole strikes, this is my alternative.

Makes
About 2 cups

Ingredients
3½ cups fresh or frozen peas (4½ pounds unshelled), thawed if using frozen

3 scallions, thinly sliced

Handful each of chopped parsley and cilantro

2 garlic cloves, coarsely chopped

1 tablespoon olive oil

2 tablespoons red wine vinegar

Salt and pepper

Method
1. Puree the peas, scallions, herbs, and garlic in a food processor, adding a tablespoon of water and slowly add enough of the olive oil to help bind the mixture. You may need to work in batches, depending on the size of your food processor.

2. Transfer the mixture from the food processor to a serving bowl and stir in the red wine vinegar, then season with salt and pepper to taste.

3. Pile into a bowl and serve with falafel, veggie burgers, or flatbread.

How does the cultivation of your favorite food impact on forests, soil, and biodiversity?

To keep pace with the demand for avocados, forests are being felled, breaking down the ecosystems that purify the air we breathe and that act as the "carbon sinks" (natural reservoirs that store carbon) we need to mitigate our carbon emissions. The more we become motivated by knowledge that our comfort is interconnected with that of the rest of nature, the more we will make different choices that help to create more regenerative systems—extending way beyond what we eat.

Green Pea Guac and Wasabi Soba

Leftover green pea guac? Repurpose it as a soba noodle sauce for a vegan meal.

Serves
2

Ingredients

1 teaspoon soy sauce

8 ounces soba noodles

1 head baby bok choy, cleaned and leaves removed from the stem

¾ cup green pea guacamole

2 tablespoons tahini (page 25)

1 tablespoon rice wine vinegar

½ tablespoon wasabi paste

1 teaspoon sesame seeds

Method

1. Prepare a bowl of iced water.

2. Bring a large saucepan of water to a boil and add the teaspoon of soy sauce. Drop in the soba noodles and bok choy and simmer, without covering the pan, for 8 minutes. Remove from the heat, drain and immediately place in the bowl of iced water.

3. Mix together the guacamole, tahini, rice wine vinegar, and wasabi paste. Drain the noodles and bok choy and mix with the sauce. Sprinkle with sesame seeds before serving.

What do you find comforting about repurposing leftovers?

Sure, I have a cleaner conscious if I don´t waste food. But the true comfort I find in repurposing leftovers comes from something deeper. When I see leftovers as tools to exercise my creativity, it opens my mind. I find the greatest comfort in embracing the freedom of not having to follow the rules of a recipe. There is a hope that comes from reminding myself of the many different ways there are to approach this world—even if I am just starting with my leftovers.

Roasted Beet and Pistachio Dip

This dip brings a splash of regal reddish purple to a picnic, and with it a reminder that your senses can trigger your instinctive ability to read the language of nature and reinforce your sense of self as a collaborator in the web of life.

Serves
10–12

Ingredients

6 beets, peeled and cut into bite-size pieces

3 garlic cloves

2 tablespoons olive oil

¾ cup shelled pistachio nuts

Zest and juice of 1 lemon

2 tablespoons tahini (page 25)

Handful of chopped mint leaves

Salt and pepper

1–2 tablespoons cold water

Method

1. Preheat the oven to 400°F. Put the beets and garlic into a baking dish and drizzle with the olive oil. Cover and roast until tender, about 40 minutes. Remove from the oven and let cool.

2. Meanwhile, if the pistachios are still in the shells, remove the shells and enjoy a few mindful moments to consider the purpose of color in nature as you work. Why do you think pistachios and beets have such signature colors?

3. Put the cooled beet and garlic, including any oil and juices, into a food processor with the lemon juice, tahini, mint, most of the pistachios, and a pinch of salt and pepper. Process and add a tablespoon or two of water to make it smoother, if necessary. Place in a serving dish, or simply pile onto lettuce, and add the remaining few chopped pistachios and the lemon zest for a contrasting color sensation.

> **How does the color of food bring you comfort?**
> Color developed as the web of life on the earth evolved. A plant that has a means of attracting animals to eat its fruit and spread its seeds will reproduce effectively. Color is an interspecies communication device. No wonder we humans find so much symbolism in color.

Knækbrød

Bread is a cornerstone of nutrition, and people needed to find ways to preserve the grain harvest as long as possible. Dried breads provide an energy throughout the lean season, especially in the high latitudes. I like to make a large batch of this recipe (knækbrød is Danish for "crisp bread"); it keeps well and is perfect for a snack or quick lunch, which, for me, is knækbrød with hummus.

Makes
About 25 crackers

Ingredients
½ cup whole oats
⅓ cup flaxseeds
⅓ cup sunflower seeds
⅓ cup pumpkin seeds
1⅔ cups stoneground white flour
1 teaspoon salt flakes
1 teaspoon baking powder
½ cup canola oil
Scant 1 cup water

Method

1. Preheat the oven to 400°F and line two baking sheets or one large baking sheet with parchment paper.

2. Mix all the dry ingredients in a bowl. Add the oil and water and mix together for 2–3 minutes.

3. Spread the dough onto the baking sheet(s), using a spatula, to about ⅛ inch thick. Bake for 15–17 minutes, until lightly golden. Cut into portions (or simply break up with your hands) while still warm.

> ### How can the sounds of eating trigger feelings of comfort?
> When I bite into knækbrød, the CRACK of seeds and grains floods my brain with nature-related thoughts. I marvel at the hardiness of seeds, I see humans foraging for grain, readying for the winter ahead, and how nature preserves them. Sound is another part of nature-related sensation.

Rainbow Tomato Salad

This refreshing tomato salad can be made with any type of tomato, but I like to use different-colored varieties, and calling it Rainbow Tomato Salad reminds me of the comfort we derive from diversity in nature.

Serves
4 as a side

Ingredients
4 handfuls of cherry tomatoes, preferably different colors, halved

3 tablespoons white wine vinegar

Salt and pepper

Handful each of freshly chopped dill and parsley

Method

1. Put the tomatoes into a bowl, mix, and marvel at the variety of colors and marbled textures. Stir in the vinegar, a dash of salt and pepper, and three-quarters of the fresh herbs. Toss and sprinkle the remaining fresh herbs on top to serve.

How do our diets reflect a human impulse to control nature?

In botanical terms, a tomato is a seed-bearing ripened ovary, making it a fruit. Yet people often think of tomatoes as vegetables. In the nineteenth century, this seemingly frivolous misunderstanding went to the U.S. Supreme Court when a tomato distributor objected to a vegetable tax (for which there was no fruit equivalent) being levied on his goods. The American Justices ruled that, because tomatoes were used primarily for savory dishes, they were legally, if not botanically, vegetables.

Preserved Tomato Sauce

Pizza, salsa, tabbouleh, tikka masala, shakshuka, baked beans, fries lathered in ketchup . . . in signature dishes around the world tomatoes provide comfort in the form of cultural identity. Making your own tomato sauce also enhances a nature-related identity.

Makes
About 4 quarts

Ingredients
14 large ripe tomatoes (about 5½ pounds), such as beefsteak tomatoes
½ cup dry red wine or vodka
1 teaspoon kosher sea salt

Method
1. Bring a large saucepan of water to a boil. Fill a large mixing bowl with iced water and put it near the stove. Cut out the stem and cut a shallow cross across the bottom of the tomatoes. Blanch by putting three tomatoes into the boiling water for 45 seconds. Remove and plunge them into a bowl of iced water. Peel off the skins (and use to make zero-waste tomato powder, see facing page) and repeat with the rest. Coarsely chop all the tomatoes.

2. Put the tomato flesh into a stockpot, add the red wine or vodka, bring to a boil, then simmer over medium heat for 1–1½ hours. Stir your sauce occasionally and take in the aroma. Look out of your window. What do you see, smell, hear, and feel? Leaves? Light? Laughter? Animals? Insects? How does it make you feel? Use your senses to make a memory.

3. Let the sauce cool and transfer to storage containers that have room for expansion as the sauce freezes. Put into the freezer—it will keep for at least three months. Then, when you want to use the sauce later in the year, take in the aroma as it warms. Do you recall any memories from the day you made the sauce? How do they make you feel? What ideas does that feeling give you about the value of preserving food?

> ### How can preserving food enhance your mental well-being?
> Practically, making and storing tomato sauce is a way to act on intent to eat with the seasons. Mentally, it exercises long-term thinking. By making preserves you are rooting yourself in a moment of seasonal transition, accepting that change is inevitable and welcoming a positive experience tomorrow. Practicing nature-related rituals with food can transform how you perceive the world and how you act in it: from head to hands to habit.

Zero-waste Tomato Powder

If you make tomato sauce, why not also make a tomato powder from the tomato skins? I am amazed at the aromatic essence of tomato that is captured in the dehydrated skins. Tomato powder adds a little of zero-waste comfort. When I use it for flavoring soups, salads, sandwich fillings, or pizza dough, I recall summer in the depths of winter, and I feel more connected to the cycle of life.

Ingredients

Tomato skins (see tomato sauce recipe, facing page)

Paprika, chili powder, or sea salt (optional)

Method

1. Lay the tomato skins on dehydrator racks or a drying rack for baked goods so that they are flat and not overlapping; an ⅛ inch of space or so between them promotes air circulation. If using a dehydrator, place the skins in the machine and turn on the vegetable setting. Check regularly but allow for 4–5 hours.

2. Alternatively, use the oven on its lowest setting. Put a single layer of the tomato skins on a wire cooling rack on top of a baking sheet and dehydrate for 5–10 hours—overnight is a good idea. Remove the skins when they are completely dry and flaky. Transfer to a coffee grinder and grind the skins until they are as fine as any other dried spice on your rack. Add a pinch of paprika, chili powder, and/or sea salt for variation. Store in an airtight jar.

> **How does creativity bring you comfort?**
> Considering everyday foods from a new perspective is stimulating because it stretches your mind. Making something inspired by a new perspective translates inspiration into positive action. This is how you can become the change.

Deviled Eggs
with Horseradish

Eating deviled eggs seasonally provides me with the comfort of being part of a collaboration with many other species. Look for eggs with deep orangey-red yolks, sourced from a local supplier—chances are those eggs were produced by free-roaming hens raised on a natural diet that includes clover, worms, grasshoppers, and spiders.

Makes
8 servings as a side

Ingredients
4 eggs
4 tablespoons quark, Greek-style yogurt, or cottage cheese
1 teaspoon grated horseradish
1 tablespoon chopped dill pickles (page 134)
Salt and pepper

To serve
Zero-waste tomato powder (page 57)
Finely chopped fresh dill

Method
1. Bring a saucepan of water to a boil, completely submerge the eggs, reduce the heat, and simmer for 12 minutes. Remove and cool the eggs under cold running water before peeling. Crush the eggshells and till into your garden (or use for houseplants) so the calcium nourishes the soil and the cycle of life continues.

2. Slice the peeled eggs in half and scoop the yolks into a bowl. Mash the yolks, stir in the quark, yogurt, or cottage cheese, the horseradish, and pickles, and season with salt and pepper. Use a spoon to refill the eggs. Serve sprinkled with tomato powder and fresh dill.

Which came first, the chicken or the egg?
Humans and chickens have a long history of coevolution, each providing the other with comfort. Chickens are special domesticated creatures, ones that have enabled us to thrive, and they deserve the same respect as the family dog.

Savory Tomato Preserves

Makes
2½ quarts or 4–6 jars, depending on size

Ingredients
3¼ pounds tomatoes, Roma is a good variety
½ cup apple juice
1 cup apple cider vinegar
1 cup honey
1½ teaspoons salt
½ teaspoon ground black pepper
½ teaspoon dry mustard
½ teaspoon ground allspice
½ teaspoon ground cumin
¼ teaspoon cayenne pepper

How can food make you feel hopeful?

Preserve making is an act that firmly roots you in a calming present moment, peppered with the expectation of comfortingly delicious moments in the future.

This tomato preserves tastes great over cream cheese or other soft cheese with crackers or knækbrød (page 54), used as a sandwich spread, served with crudités, or as a condiment on a cheeseboard.

Method

1. Before you make any preserves, always sterilize your equipment. You can sterilize glass jars by one of the following ways. Bring a large saucepan full of water to a boil and completely submerge the jars, lids, and rings (if using). Let boil for 10 minutes, then carefully remove and place the jars on a clean surface and let dry.

2. Alternatively, place the washed jars on a baking sheet and put them into the oven preheated to 225°F for 10 minutes. You will need a large saucepan of boiling water to seal the jars, so if you use method 1, keep the pan of water handy for this purpose.

3. To make the preserves, first skin and peel your tomatoes (page 56). Set aside the skins for making tomato powder (page 57). Coarsely chop the flesh, then put the chopped tomatoes, with all their juices, into a bowl. Set aside.

4. Combine all the other ingredients in a large saucepan over medium heat, stirring until the honey dissolves. Add the reserved tomatoes and juices and bring to a boil. Reduce the heat to a simmer, and let the tomatoes cook until the mixture is reduced by half. The slow heat helps to develop the sugars in the tomatoes, so don't try to rush this stage.

5. Now, seal the jars to prevent bacteria being introduced to the preserves. Fill the sterilized jars, leaving a ¼-inch headspace, and screw the lids on tightly. Submerge the jars into a saucepan of boiling water, using tongs; work in batches, if necessary, and make sure the jars are completely submerged and not touching each other. Boil for 10 minutes and remove with tongs. Set the jars aside to cool, and 24 hours later test the seal by putting pressure on the lid with your finger. If it gives, the processing didn't completely seal the jar and you should refrigerate it and use within a week. If the lid does not give, your preserves should be fine stored in a cool dark place for up to a year.

Tomato and Corn Pie

Serves
6–8

Ingredients

1⅔ cups all-purpose flour, plus extra for dusting

½ teaspoon sugar

½ teaspoon salt

¼ teaspoon ground black pepper

1 stick (4 ounces) butter, cubed and softened, plus extra for greasing

½ teaspoon fresh thyme leaves

2–3 tablespoons iced water

For the filling

2 beefsteak tomatoes or 3 large tomatoes

3 eggs

1 cup milk

1 teaspoon fresh thyme leaves

1 cup fresh corn kernels (removed from 2 corn cobs)

2 scallions, thinly sliced

1 cup shredded vegetarian cheddar cheese

Salt and ground black pepper

Tomatoes were once viewed with fear and superstition. Early British settlers in North America grew them only as ornamentals, not to eat. During the American Civil War, fact overcame fiction when tomatoes were canned to feed people whose lands had been destroyed. Postwar, dishes such as tomato soup eventually won over the hearts, minds, and taste buds of people who found superstition hard to let go. This tomato and corn pie would surely have met with approval.

Method

1. Sift together the flour, sugar, salt, and pepper into a bowl. Cut the butter into the dry ingredients with two knives, using a crisscross motion, or rub in with your fingers until the mixture resembles bread crumbs. Add the thyme leaves and the iced water, a couple of teaspoonfuls at a time. You want the dough to bind but not be runny. With floured hands, take the dough out of the bowl and form it into a disk. Put the dough onto a plate, cover with a dish towel, and chill in the refrigerator for 30 minutes.

2. Grease and line a pie dish or 9-inch tart pan. Remove the dough from the refrigerator, place on a floured surface, and roll into a circle large enough to line the tart pan. Press the dough into the pan and chill for another 30 minutes.

3. Preheat the oven to 400°F. Line the dough with parchment paper, fill with pie weights or dried beans, and bake for 10 minutes. Remove the pie weights and paper, return to the oven, and bake for another 10 minutes, until the pastry is golden and crisp. Set aside while you make the filling.

4. Skin and peel the tomatoes (page 56). Keep the skins for making tomato powder (page 57). Seed and slice the tomatoes into ¼ inch slices.

5. Beat the eggs and add the milk, thyme, salt, and pepper. Put a layer of tomato slices into the pastry shell, followed by most of the corn kernels, most of the scallions, and most of the cheese. Pour the egg mixture evenly over the filling and arrange the remaining tomato slices, corn, scallions, and cheese on top. Bake for 30 minutes, or until the filling is set and a knife emerges clean from the center. Serve immediately while sharing the story of the tomato.

Why do your food preferences change as your life changes?

If discouragement strikes, take comfort in the history of the tomato and how it is a reminder that change is possible.

Zucchini Canoes

Serves
4

Ingredients
½ cup bulgur wheat

⅔ cup boiling water

3 medium tomatoes

2 large zucchini

1½ tablespoons olive oil

1 small onion, finely chopped

2 garlic cloves, minced

¾ cup rinsed and drained
canned chickpeas

1 small carrot, diced

2 dried apricots, sliced (or use
fresh ones, pitted)

1¼ cups vegetable broth
(page 108)

¼ teaspoon ground cinnamon

½ teaspoon ground coriander

½ teaspoon ground ginger

½ teaspoon ground turmeric

¼ cup pitted olives

2 tablespoons golden raisins

Freshly chopped cilantro

Salt and ground black pepper

As a child, I knew it was zucchini season when our neighbor, Harold Handyside, laid green bundles of joy from his garden on our doorstep. Today, I like to bake zucchini in the form of canoes that hint at the Native Americans who nurtured squash way before Harold. I always make extra stuffing when preparing this dish— useful for lunches later in the week.

Method

1. Preheat the oven to 400°F. Put the bulgur wheat into a bowl, pour in the water, cover the bowl, and set aside for 10–15 minutes until the water is absorbed. Fluff up with a fork.

2. Meanwhile, cut out the stem and cut a cross on the bottom of each tomato. Blanch by putting them in a bowl of boiling water for about 45 seconds. Remove and plunge them into a bowl of iced water. Peel off the skins (use to make tomato powder, page 57) and chop the tomatoes.

3. Slice the zucchini in half lengthwise. Use a spoon to carefully scoop out the flesh (don't break the skins), chop, and set aside. Lay the hollowed "canoes" side by side in a baking dish and drizzle with 1½ teaspoons of the oil.

4. Heat the remaining olive oil in a large saucepan over medium heat and sauté the onions for 5–7 minutes. Add the garlic and, after a minute, mix in the zucchini and tomato flesh, chickpeas, carrots, apricots, broth, spices, olives, and raisins. Give everything a stir, season, and simmer for 20 minutes. Add the bulgur to the pan and simmer for another 10–15 minutes, until the broth has evaporated. Divide the mixture among the zucchini canoes. Bake for 25–30 minutes. Serve warm, sprinkled with cilantro.

> **What nonfood related memories are triggered when you eat?**
> When I eat zucchini in summer, my mind is flooded with thoughts that extend far beyond the table. Like humans, zucchini prefer warm soil, full sun, and, being reliant upon bees for pollination, a life among a community of flowers to increase their ability to fertilize their seeds. It's a joyful connection to the cycle of life.

Zucchini "Pasta" Bowls

"Pasta" using vegetables is a lighter alternative to traditional spaghetti or noodles. This recipe teams zucchini with asparagus, which means it is meant as an early summer bowl of nature-related comfort. If you make it later in the summer, simply omit the no longer seasonal asparagus and experiment with whatever is in season.

Serves
4

Ingredients
8 shallots, minced
1¾ sticks (7 ounces) butter, at room temperature
Zest and juice of 1 lemon
1½ cups bulgur wheat
2 cups boiling water
1–2 zucchini
½ cup oats
1 bunch asparagus, thinly sliced
20 cherry tomatoes, halved
⅔ cup fresh shelled peas
Handful each of chopped parsley and mint

Method
1. Mix the shallots, butter, and lemon zest together. Put the bulgur wheat into a bowl, add the boiling water, cover the bowl with a cloth, and set aside for 10–15 minutes, until fluffy, then mix a tablespoon of the shallot butter into the bulgur.

2. Thinly slice the zucchini into ribbons using a Y-shape vegetable peeler, then slice the ribbons lengthwise.

3. Toast the oats in a dry saucepan over low heat for 7 minutes, stirring until lightly brown. Transfer to a plate and, in the same pan, use a tablespoon of shallot butter to sauté the zucchini, asparagus, tomatoes, and peas. Evenly distribute the bulgur and vegetables in bowls, top with the oats, and drizzle with the lemon juice. Sprinkle with herbs and serve.

How do you connect to soil through food?
When local zucchini appear on market stalls, it is a sign that the soil has been warmed enough by the sun to trigger growth. Pause and consider the weather as you shop. Has it been moderately warm or unusually hot? How much rain has fallen? How has that impacted on the soil and growing season? How have the conditions affected the local foods available? Do you have the same weather preferences as your zucchini?

Crispy Bean Salad

I often mix a large batch of this salad when I know I will be too busy or too lazy to cook. I like to team fava beans with fresh snow peas of the season to make a salad that keeps for several days in the refrigerator. On the surface, these are legumes that grow quietly all summer, while below ground they work in harmony with bacteria to feed the life that swings into action in this most fertile of seasons. Fava beans are left to dry on the stem to be harvested in fall. Once they have fed the soil, they provide us with a shelf-stable protein source to last the year.

Serves
6–8

Ingredients
⅔ cup dried fava beans (or other dried bean, such as lima beans), soaked overnight

1 cup pearl barley

1½ cups snow peas, chopped into thirds

4–6 spring onions, thinly sliced

1 cup coarsely chopped baby spinach

Handful of freshly chopped soft herbs (such as parsley, chervil, or dill)

Small handful of sunflower seeds

½ cup olive oil

Salt and pepper

For the dressing
2 teaspoons red wine vinegar

2 teaspoons Dijon mustard

1 tablespoon drained and chopped capers

¼ cup olive oil

Method
1. Put the soaked and drained beans into a saucepan and cover with fresh water. Bring to a boil, then reduce heat and simmer for 1 hour before draining. Set aside to cool.

2. Meanwhile put the barley into a separate saucepan with 2 cups of water. Bring to a boil and simmer for 30 minutes or until the barley has absorbed the water. Remove from the heat and cool.

3. Prepare the dressing by mixing the vinegar, mustard, and capers. Slowly whisk in the olive oil to create an emulsion.

4. Toss the snow peas, scallions, spinach, and herbs with the sunflower seeds and oil in a large bowl. Season, then stir in the cooled beans and barley. Pour in the dressing and toss again before serving.

How in tune are your actions with those of the life that surrounds you?
I love this thought, because I find myself alternating between racing around and simply soaking up the sun in the summer. In many ways, when we humans give ourselves over to this pace of life, we are mirroring the symphonic chaos of the world around as it absorbs and shares the energy from the sun.

Peas in a Pod Salad

Awww, shucks! Some tasks are a pleasure in themselves, far more than simply a means to an end. So take a few comforting moments to sit down and shuck your peas. Here's a delicious salad to make when peas in the pod are in season. Serve warm from the pan.

Method

1. Split the pea pods with your thumbs and run your finger along the inside of the shells to remove the peas straight into a bowl.

2. Put the barley into a saucepan with 2 cups of water. Bring to a boil and simmer for 30 minutes or until the barley has absorbed the water. Remove from the heat.

3. Melt half the coconut oil in a saucepan, add the garlic and a pinch of salt, and sauté for 3 minutes. Add the peas and cook for 4 minutes. Add the remaining coconut butter, the lettuce, and seasoning, and remove from the heat when the lettuce has wilted. Mix in the barley and parsley. Toss and serve.

Serves
4

Ingredients
1 pounds fresh peas in their shells

1 cup pearl barley

¼ cup coconut oil

3 garlic cloves, finely chopped

2 Little Gem lettuce heads, leaves separated, hearts removed

Salt and pepper

Coarsely chopped parsley, to garnish (optional)

How did the phrase "like peas in a pod" develop?

Pause for a moment and consider the first humans who looked at peas nestled in a pod and thought, these peas symbolize the best relationships. I find comfort in common phrases that demonstrate how human culture mirrors nature. Perhaps we are not so disconnected after all?

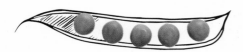

Savory Pickled Plum and Kale Salad

This recipe weaves in a few pickling skills and pairs hardy kale with the ripe plums of late summer for a tangy meal. I like to serve it as a main with a big spoonful of hummus, a couple of slices of cheese, or some tofu.

Serves

4

Ingredients

For the pickled plums

½ cup water

½ cup red wine vinegar

½ cup sugar or maple syrup

Pinch of salt

8 plums, pitted and quartered

For the salad

12 large curly kale leaves, central woody stems removed

2 tablespoons extra virgin olive oil

Salt and pepper

Roasted pumpkin seeds (page 160), to garnish

For the dressing

2 tablespoons pickling liquid

3 tablespoons extra virgin olive oil

1 tablespoon maple syrup

1 teaspoon fresh thyme leaves

Pinch of salt and pepper

Method

1. Put the pickling ingredients, minus the plums, into a small saucepan and heat until the sugar has dissolved. Remove from the heat, add the plums, coat in the liquid, and set aside for 30 minutes.

2. Preheat the oven to 400°F. Massage the kale leaves with olive oil for 10 minutes to break down the cellular structure, making the leaves more chewable. Put the kale onto a baking sheet in a single layer, season, and put into the oven for 4 minutes. Flip and bake for another 3 minutes to crisp on both sides.

3. Make the dressing by combining 2 tablespoons of the pickling liquid with the other ingredients, whisk, and season.

4. Pile the kale leaves, plums, and dressing on serving plates and sprinkle with pumpkin seeds.

What questions come to mind when you consider food from the perspectives of water, soil, and air?

Kale from the human perspective is a superfood full of healthy fiber, calcium, and antioxidants. But what stories can be told about kale when considered from the perspective of water, soil, and air? The adaptable kale can grow in different climates and soil. It gets thirsty, but because it can thrive in colder climates, it grows in places less dependent upon irrigation. Frost turns the kale's starch into sugar, making it tastier and a great alternative to imported fresh produce.

Strawberry Chips

Summer and strawberries are synonymous! In fact, the Oneida Native American tribe's word for June is strawberry. Making strawberry chips is my favorite way to preserve love for living seasonally, because they dry in the shape of hearts. What was that I wrote earlier about comfort food being a craving for love?

Ingredients

Strawberries, washed, hulled, and dried

Method

1. Slice your strawberries thinly and evenly. Place the slices on dehydrator trays or cooling racks, leaving a ¼ inch gap between them. If you have a dehydrator, place them in the machine and turn on the fruit setting. Check regularly and remove when they are completely dry.

2. Alternatively, place the racks on a baking sheet and put them in the oven on its lowest setting. Either method should take 8–10 hours. Cool before storing in airtight containers—they will keep for up to a year.

> ### How does the shape of food bring you comfort?
> Just as your brain perceives anything from elephants to eggplants in the shape of the clouds, we also perceive comforting objects in the shape of food. That is one reason why many foods are considered to be aphrodisiacs..

Strawberry Crisp Muesli

This simple recipe is designed to help you start your day with some nature-related reflection. Why not serve the muesli with homemade peanut milk? See the recipe on page 86.

Makes
10 servings

Ingredients
½ cup hazelnuts
3 cups rolled oats
½ cup strawberry chips
(see recipe facing page)
½ cup coconut flakes
½ cup pumpkin seeds
¼ cup chia seeds
¼ teaspoon salt

Method
1. Preheat the oven to 300°F. Spread the hazelnuts on a large baking sheet and put into the oven for 5 minutes.

2. Remove the baking sheet, add the oats, then return to the oven and bake for another 10 minutes. Remove, let cool, and mix in the remaining ingredients. Store in an airtight container for up to a month. Serve with milk.

Tip
For a Bircher-style muesli, mix 1 cup of muesli with 1 cup of milk and 1 tablespoon of maple syrup, cover, and soak overnight.

How do daily food rituals help you identify as a part of nature?

Breakfast is a great time to weave a nature-related ritual into your life. Each morning, particularly if the weather is not your favorite, consider how it might be a comfort (or an endurance) for other forms of life upon which you are dependent. Routinely pausing to think from another life-form´s perspective will develop your language of nature fluency.

Strawberry Preserves

Strawberry season offers another moment to spend an afternoon preserving in your kitchen with one foot firmly planted in the present, and another giving thought to the future. How about a nod to the past as well? Legend has it that a French spy on a mission in the eighteenth century took Chilean cuttings back to France to cross with the strawberries common in Europe. The French tried to keep the results a secret, but word got out and a berry craze ensued.

Makes

3 (9¾-ounce) jars

Ingredients

2¼ pounds fresh strawberries

2 ½ cups sugar

3 tablespoons plus 1 teaspoon pectin powder

1 tablespoon apple cider vinegar

Method

1. First sterilize the jars and lids as described on page 60.

2. Hull your berries by cutting off the leafy tops as well as the white flesh immediately below. It's easiest to do this by holding a pointed sharp knife at an angle and cutting in a circular motion.

3. Put the strawberries, sugar, pectin, and vinegar into a saucepan and mash them to a thick pulp. Bring to a boil, then reduce the heat and simmer for 5 minutes. Skim off any foam that accumulates on the surface. After 15 minutes, divide the preserves evenly among your jars, leaving a ¼-inch headspace. Screw the lids on tightly. Process the preserves as described on page 60 to keep the jars shelf stable for up to a year.

> **What comfort can we derive from eating certain foods only when they are in season?**
>
> As you make the preserves, look out the window. What do you see and hear? How does the air feel on your skin? Reflect and use your senses to make a summer memory. When you eat your preserves in winter see whether they trigger those sensual memories.

Blueberry Cobbler

For me, the color of this dessert represents summer itself. Like the color, its taste, too, is rare: a little sweet, a little tart, the flavor of the earth. You can use whichever berries you prefer, such as raspberries, strawberries, or blackberries, or even cherries, but pause and give thought to how the color of the fruit changes your perspective of the dish.

Serves
6

Ingredients

½ cup granulated sugar

1 teaspoon ground cinnamon

1 teaspoon ground cardamom

1 teaspoon salt

5¼ cups blueberries (do not thaw if using frozen)

1 tablespoon apple cider vinegar

For the cobbler

1¼ cups all-purpose flour

½ cup granulated sugar, plus extra for sprinkling

1½ teaspoons baking powder

¼ teaspoon salt

1 stick (4 ounces) unsalted butter (to make your own, see page 156), plus extra for greasing

½ cup heavy cream (or, if you make your own butter, use the buttermilk here)

½ teaspoon vanilla extract

Method

1. Preheat the oven to 375°F and grease an 8-inch square baking dish.

2. Mix together the sugar, cinnamon, cardamom, and salt. Stir in the blueberries to coat with the mix, then add the vinegar before you transfer the fruit to the baking dish.

3. Sift together the flour, sugar, baking powder, and salt. Melt the butter over low heat and add the cream and vanilla extract to the pan. Combine the wet and dry ingredients and mix to a dough. Use an ice cream scoop or spoon to place nine evenly spaced scoops of dough on top of the blueberries.

4. Sprinkle with 2 teaspoons of sugar and bake in the oven for 35–40 minutes. Let the cobbler cool for 15–20 minutes before serving.

Tip By freezing blueberries, you can make this dish all year. Rinse and dry the berries. Put the berries onto a baking sheet lined with parchment paper, aiming to keep them separate. Put into the freezer for 3 hours. Store the berries in an airtight container for up to a year. Use from frozen.

> **Which colors in food are you most drawn to and why?**
> Blue-colored life is rare, because it requires an unusual combination of chemistry, energy, and light-reflecting surfaces. I find comfort in the calm of blue and the fire of red represented in the colors of a blueberry cobbler.

Ritual

Brandied Cherries

Makes
2 (18-ounce) jars

Ingredients
3¼ cups pitted cherries
1 cup water
⅓ cup sugar
1 cinnamon stick, broken
in half
1 vanilla bean, split lengthwise
and seeds scraped
Pinch of freshly grated nutmeg
4 juniper berries, smashed
1 star anise, broken in half
1¼ cups brandy

The bing in a Badda Bing martini (page 78) is the brandied cherry.
This is a beautifully versatile garnish to be used with great creativity.
I also use them as the center for homemade chocolate truffles.
A small jar makes a wonderful gift, too.

Method
1. First sterilize the jars and lids as described on page 60.
Pack the cherries into the jars, leaving a ½-inch headspace.

2. Put the water, sugar, and spices into a medium saucepan
and bring to a simmer. Once the sugar has dissolved, remove
from the heat and let steep for 15 minutes.

3. Strain the liquid to remove the spice pieces. Add the brandy
and pour over the cherries so that they are submerged.

4. Process following the method on page 60. The flavor will be
most intense after 2–3 months, if you can wait that long!

What is comforting about making food from scratch?

Making preserves from raw foods reinforces your position in the food web, particularly when you play a role in the magical transformation to a long-lasting food stuff. You may introduce cherries to sugar, but together they do the preserving work.

Badda Bing Martini

Nature relatedness aside, I'm a sucker for a 1950s-style martini. Simple, organic vodkas are great sustainable cocktail choices, because the purest water depends on the purest water sources. The relaxing connectedness to be supped after mindfully making the preserves to pull this cocktail together definitely adds some badda bing to a warm summer's evening.

Serves
1

Ingredients
2 tablespoons cherry syrup (see below)

¼ cup your favorite vodka or gin

A few mint leaves

A brandied cherry (page 76), to decorate

For the cherry syrup
2½ cups fresh pitted cherries

⅓ cup sugar

Method

1. First make the syrup. Wash the cherries and put them and the sugar into a saucepan over medium heat. Bring to a boil and simmer for about 10 minutes, then mash to release the juices.

2. Remove from the heat and pour through a strainer set over a bowl. Pour the syrup into a clean bottle and keep in the refrigerator for up to ten days—it makes enough for several cocktails.

3. To make the martini, fill a cocktail shaker with ice. Add the cherry syrup and vodka or gin to the shaker with a few mint leaves. Cover and shake!

4. Rub the rim of a chilled martini glass with a piece of mint to release the oils. Strain the chilled mixture into a martini glass, top with a dash of water, a mint leaf, and a brandied cherry.

> **How do our creature comforts connect with those of other creatures?**
> We are not the only life-form attracted to red, and planting red flowers will attract some feathered friends to your yard, where they prune and pollinate. When birds munch cherry buds, they thin out the excess blooms and in doing so they help trees redirect their energy, resulting in fewer but plumper cherries. The Badda Bing martini is a preserved celebration of color and collaboration with which to raise a comforting glass.

The Good Ship (Cherry) Lollipop

Here's a modern take on the classic Shirley Temple for those craving a virgin cocktail made using the preserved bounty of summer.

Method

1. Fill a cocktail shaker and a tall glass with ice. Add the cherry syrup and grenadine to the cocktail shaker and shake. Strain into the glass and top with ginger ale. Garnish with a slice of lime or orange.

Serves
1

Ingredients
1½ teaspoons cherry syrup (see recipe facing page)

1½ teaspoons grenadine syrup

Ginger ale

Lime or orange slices, to garnish

Ice

> **How does food help you cultivate joy?**
> Raise a glass to the comfort found in the diversity of nature. As you drink, let yourself be filled with love for your part in the web of life.

Eating
for
Creativity

Cultivating Fluency in the Language of Nature

In 1968, speaking about social change as part of his campaign for U.S. presidential nomination, Robert F. Kennedy quoted George Bernard Shaw:

"Some men see things as they are and ask why. I dream of things that never were, and ask why not."

When I was an idealistic teenager with those words pinned on my wall, I thought the point was to dream up the "why nots." Now, I think asking "why" is just as important. Both require creativity.

We live in an age called the Anthropocene, an epoch of human dominion over all other forms of life and the elements upon which we all depend, and that has resulted in climate change. Increasingly, we are becoming aware that economic, social, and environmental justice are interlinked. It is a sign that our systems need to change and we have a whole lot of "why nots" to dream up. But if we want those "why nots" to help us create a regenerative world, one that is fair for all forms of life, we also have to look at why we humans adopted a mindset that caused all this mess in the first place. Climate-change solutions are human solutions, and to find them, we all need to exercise our creativity.

Exercising creativity makes you feel good. The Hungarian-American psychologist Mihaly Csikszentmihalyi, author of *Creativity: The Psychology of Discovery and Invention*, put it this way:

"Creativity is the central source of meaning in our lives … most of the things that are interesting, important, and human are the results of creativity … when we are involved in it, we feel that we are living more fully than during the rest of life."

Let's find our creative flow as a part of nature, with food.

Linking Environmental and Social Justice

Since World War II, the main food question we have asked is: How do we make more? The predominant answer to that question has been monocrop production, which requires breaking down diverse ecosystems to support the life of one species. The problem is that all life is part of a web that thrives in relation to the life and death of other life-forms. So, in our pursuit of food security, we have made our food system insecure, because we have broken down the ecosystem it relies on. The World Wildlife Fund's *Living Planet Index* indicates that our actions are hastening the extinction of other forms of live at an increasing rate. Over the past fifty years, our collective destructive ecological footprint has increased by 190 percent. As in fashion, could less actually be more?

In the 1980s, the Indian economist Amartya Sen won a Nobel Prize for his work revealing how food security is more about distribution than production. Taking food that is produced for animal feed out the equation, each person on the earth has an allocation of about 2,800 calories per day from current production levels. Depending on your gender and activity levels, health guidelines recommend eating between 2,000 and 2,500 calories. We produce more than enough food to feed everyone in the world. True food security lies in solutions that promote environmental and social justice and that require growing food regeneratively and wasting less of what we have.

Creativity is the central source of meaning in our lives

Discovering Collective Value

If "food waste" was a nation, it would be third to the United States and China in terms of greenhouse gas emissions. How do we stop? "Waste" is those things we don't perceive to be valuable. Increasing the value of food in our lives is the first step to changing our behavior. The more we learn about the food web, the more we realize that nothing exists in nature if it doesn't have value. To appreciate the value of the food web, we have to look at it beyond the human perspective.

This chapter takes a creative approach to increase the value of the food web in your eating life. There are top tips on food waste and eating locally during winter, but also beginner's mind questions and rituals that help you tell new stories about yourself as nature. Life itself is an act of creation.

Ritual

Creativity Rituals with Food: Nature Relatedness in the Lean Season

The lean season refers to those months during the growing cycle, when we are farthest from the harvest. Traditionally, the pantry would have been becoming bare and people would be eagerly awaiting the return of fresh fruit and vegetables in late spring. I live in Denmark, a country that has been inhabited by humans for thousands of years. From our twenty-first-century perspective, we might think that relying on local and seasonal foods in the lean season is difficult, but it is clearly possible.

Lean-season local eating is an opportunity for creative nature relatedness. Necessity is the mother of invention. And our necessity is twofold: first, to align mind, body, and habit to nature's harmony and, second, to change not only ourselves as individuals but our collective systems. The recipes that follow are designed to do both as you increase your lean-season creativity.

Ritual

Creativity Ritual with Nature: How to Read a Tree

There was a time when humans worshipped trees. Considering that we wouldn't breathe or eat were it not for trees, I think this is a reasonable world view. What can you learn about the value of food and nature from trees? Pick a tree that you see on a regular basis and make a habit of paying attention to it. You will notice big things, perhaps the loss of its leaves before winter. What about the details? Do the leaves hang the same way morning, noon, and night? Does it produce fruit? Does the amount of fruit vary from year to year? Do certain animals live in the tree? If so, how is the relationship mutually beneficial? What about those elements you cannot see? Where do the tree's roots run? How does that affect the soil?

Year in, year out, your tree is communicating with its environment and making decisions about how to live, depending on what changes around it. It becomes creative in order to adapt to its environment so that it can thrive. What can you learn from your tree about how food is connected to all of nature? Can you find any lessons on creative freedom, in treedom?

Parsley and Walnut Pesto

Pesto comes from a Genoese word meaning "to crush," and eating for creativity calls for crushing rules if they don't serve us—such as how we make pesto. Most pesto recipes call for pine nuts, but let's emphasize variation, reduce our overreliance on one source, and promote biodiversity in nature by promoting biodiversity in our diet. Balance is the key to the good life. That is why I offer you three different vegan twists on classic pesto.

Makes

Enough for 4 servings of pasta or gnocchi

Ingredients

4 garlic cloves

20 walnuts in the shell

2 large bunches of parsley, stems and leaves, chopped

Scant ½ cup olive oil

Salt and pepper

Method

1. Pound the garlic using a mortar and pestle until it becomes a paste. Crack open the walnuts, break the nuts into small chunks with your hands, and rub them firmly with the pestle against the side of the mortar, releasing the oils. Add the parsley, handful by handful, until you have a coarse green paste. As you work, add small pinches of salt, which acts as an abrasive. If you are pressed for time, put all the ingredients into your food processor. Or, if you have 20 minutes to spare, take time connecting with the texture and aroma of your ingredients and consider your exchange with the mini ecosystem in your mortar and pestle.

2. When you have a coarse paste, begin to add the olive oil a tablespoon or so at a time—keep crushing until the pesto is the consistency you prefer.

Why might it be worthwhile to add a twist to a traditional dish?

Pesto and pine nuts go hand in hand, yet most pine nuts reach market by way of sweeping forest floors completely clear of these nuggets of nourishment that feed birds and animals, bio-organic material that feeds soil and seeds that regenerates tree population. Rethinking how we honor the ecosystem of trees in our favorite recipes is a creative way to look after your own well-being.

Variation: Cilantro and Hazelnut Pesto

Hazel trees are a drought-resistant, not water-intensive crop. They thrive in marginal soil, making hazelnuts friends of easily degradable soil. I team them with cilantro, a herb that has been found in 5,000-year-old burial sites, because I think the pairing reinforces the understanding that human resilience has always been dependent upon all forms of life.

Method

1. Follow the main recipe, but use hazelnuts instead of walnuts, cilantro instead of parsley, and half hazelnut oil and half canola oil instead of the olive oil.

Variation: Basil and Brazil Nut Pesto

Brazil nuts grow in rain forests and don't like cultivation. They rely on the biodiversity of the forest, the flora of which attracts a specific bee to pollinate the tree. Maintaining a market for Brazil nuts helps to sustain rain forests, because they are not a food that can be transitioned into a monocrop for which native forests are felled.

Method

1. Follow the main recipe, but use Brazil nuts instead of walnuts, and basil instead of parsley.

Peanut Butter

Peanuts are legumes not nuts, plants with nitrogen-fixing properties. All plants take nitrogen from the soil, but when legumes decompose, they feed carbon and nitrogen into the soil. What better lean-season food with which to practice nature relatedness to fuel your creativity?

Makes
About 1 cup

Ingredients
5 cups unshelled peanuts (about 1 pound)
1 teaspoon table salt
1 tablespoon honey (optional)

Method
1. Sit down with two bowls, one for your shells, one for your peanuts, and spend 30 minutes shelling. Reserve the shells.

2. Put the peanuts, salt, and honey (if using) into a food processor. Blend for 7 minutes, pausing periodically to scrape down the sides. Transfer your butter to a clean jar and store in a cool dry cupboard for up to three months. Now reflect on how you are part of the cycle of life by harvesting the nitrogen in the shells. Crush to a mulch and add to your garden, houseplants, or local park to feed the soil.

Peanut Milk

Vegan nut milk is no twenty-first century invention. A hundred years ago, George Washington Carver, director of agriculture at the Tuskegee Institute, Alabama, promoted exercising creativity by making peanut milk. As he said: "When you can do common things in life in an uncommon way, you will command the attention of the world."

Makes
3⅓ cups

Ingredients
¾ cup shelled peanuts, soaked overnight
4¼ cups water
1 teaspoon honey (optional)

Method
1. Rinse the soaked peanuts, drain, and transfer to a blender. Add the water and honey for a sweeter milk. Blend for 3 minutes. Pour into a strainer lined with cheesecloth (or a nut bag) set over a bowl. Squeeze the pulp in the cloth to drain the milk. Store in the refrigerator for up to three days. Now, what to do with the nut pulp?

Zero-waste Peanut Pulp Crackers

One man's garbage is another man's treasure; "waste" is a matter of perspective. Peanut pulp is what you created by making peanut milk. Instead of being waste, pulp is a binding agent that can lay the foundations for another creation that adds value to your life. Reforming your thoughts reforms your words, which in turn reforms your actions—like piling pesto onto these peanut pulp crackers.

Makes
About 30 small crackers

Ingredients
Peanut pulp from making peanut milk (see facing page)

1 tablespoon sesame seeds, plus extra for sprinkling

½ teaspoon salt

2 tablespoons whole-wheat flour

1–2 tablespoons water

Zaatar (optional)

Method

1. Preheat the oven to 400°F and line a baking sheet with parchment paper.

2. Mix the peanut pulp, seeds, salt, and flour together. Stir in a tablespoon of water. If you have a spreadable consistency, you're done; if not, add another tablespoon of water.

3. Transfer your dough to the lined baking sheet and roll into a rectangle about ⅛ inch thick. Sprinkle some seeds or spice, such as zaatar, on top. Bake for 30–35 minutes, keeping a close eye on them. Remove from the oven when brown. Cut into pieces while still warm.

What value do peanuts add to nature, beyond feeding humans?

George Washington Carver (1864–1943) was born into slavery in North America. When slavery was abolished, his drive to move the South away from intensive cotton farming led President Franklin Roosevelt to honor him for his creative vision to promote social and environmental justice. Carver saw that reliance on a cash crop contributed to divisive economics and a culture of dominance. He also saw that monocropping was stripping life from the soil on which everyone depended. His muse for justice? The peanut. Carver set out to harness the peanut's power of creation and devised more than a hundred ways of using the peanut that would build a market for peanut farming.

Veggie Stir-Fry with Peanut Butter Sauce

The lean season, when fewer foods are available fresh, is a great time to experiment, because it forces you to think about your local environment. Here is a peanut butter stir-fry made primarily with preserved local ingredients befitting the lean season. If you can't get a squash, why not substitute carrots? Use whatever noodles you have in the cupboard: rice noodles, soba noodles, spaghetti, linguine—try them!

Serves
4

Ingredients
10 ounces noodles

1 onion, sliced

¼ small butternut squash, peeled, seeded, and cut into bite-size pieces

2 cups sliced red cabbage

3 garlic cloves, minced

2 teaspoons freshly grated ginger

Cilantro or basil leaves, to garnish

For the sauce
1 tablespoon sesame oil

1 tablespoon soy sauce

1 tablespoon sweet chili sauce

1 tablespoon apple molasses (page 171) or maple syrup

⅓ cup peanut butter (page 86)

1 tablespoon apple cider vinegar

Method
1. Whisk together the sauce ingredients and set aside.

2. Boil the noodles in a saucepan of salted water according to the package directions.

3. Meanwhile, warm the oil in a large skillet or wok, add the onion, and sauté for 2–3 minutes before adding the squash. Stir-fry and let it soften for 6 minutes, then add in the cabbage, garlic, and ginger. Continue to stir-fry for 5 minutes.

4. Drain the noodles and add them to the pan. Use tongs to combine everything. Then pour over the peanut sauce and mix so that the noodles and vegetables are completely coated. Add a few cilantro or basil leaves before serving.

> **What stops you from improvising in the kitchen?**
> I am often asked how I eat local, seasonal, and organic foods when a recipe calls for something else? My answer is: change the recipe.

Jerusalem Artichoke Risotto

There is debate over when humans transitioned from collecting wild rice to growing it, but it was at least 6,000 years ago. Arborio rice is a type of short-grain rice grown since medieval times in northern Italy and used to make a signature dish: risotto. For a vegan version, simply omit the goat cheese and add another drizzle of olive oil.

Serves
4

Ingredients

1 pound Jerusalem artichokes, well washed

3 garlic cloves

¼ cup olive oil

2¾ cups vegetable broth (page 108) or 1 bouillon cube

2 small onions, finely chopped

2 celery sticks, thinly sliced

⅔ cup frozen peas

1⅓ cups Arborio rice or other risotto rice

Scant 1 cup vermouth or dry white wine

⅔ cup crumbled goat cheese (skin removed)

2 tablespoons capers (optional)

Salt

Fresh thyme leaves, to serve

Method

1. Peel and quarter the artichokes. Put them with the garlic into a saucepan of water, bring to a boil, then simmer for 15 minutes. Drain, reserving the water. Transfer the artichokes and garlic to a bowl with half the olive oil and mash with a little salt to a puree.

2. If you aren't using homemade vegetable broth, measure 2¾ cups of the reserved water and dissolve a bouillon cube in it.

3. Heat the remaining olive oil in a saucepan. Add the onion and celery and let soften for 2 minutes over low heat. Add the peas and then the rice. Quickly pour in the vermouth or wine. Breathe in the aroma as the rice absorbs the wine and the liquid reduces. Then spoon in the vegetable broth, one ladleful at a time, and stir until absorbed, repeating until all the broth has been used—this takes 20 minutes.

4. Stir in the artichoke, goat cheese, and capers (if using). Turn off the heat, cover, and let sit for 3 minutes before serving with a sprinkling of fresh thyme.

How can our relationship with rice inspire creativity?

The domestication of plants such as rice led to the foundation of civilizations. Cultivating rice meant creating irrigation and drainage systems; building bridges, canals, terraces, and storage; developing distribution and transport links; and organizing labor, trade, and keeping records. However, yields are falling due to land and water scarcity in some parts of the world and rising temperatures, sea level, and rainfall in others. It's time to reframe our relationship with rice. Should we be less concerned with rice yields and focus on more biodiverse diets? Creative solutions have the potential to change our food systems and our societies. Something to chew on while you stir this risotto.

Oatmeal Honey Bread

Once considered horse fodder, simple, wholesome, unassuming oats make delicious bread that can be turned out in less than 40 minutes. This recipe requires you to grind rolled oats into flour, a ritual intended for you to insert yourself at an earlier stage in the bread-making process than normal and give you a chance to ponder how oats, horses, and other creatures are our creative partners.

Makes

1 (9 x 5-inch) loaf

Ingredients

3⅓ cups rolled oats

½ teaspoon baking powder

1 teaspoon baking soda

2 teaspoons ground cinnamon

2 eggs

⅔ cup honey

1 cup peanut milk (page 86) or oat milk

½ teaspoon salt

Handful of strawberry chips (page 72), or nuts, seeds, or other dried fruit

Method

1. Preheat the oven to 350°F. Grease and line a 9 by 5-inch loaf pan with parchment paper.

2. Put the rolled oats into a food processor and grind for 2 minutes until you have flour. Add the baking powder, baking soda, and cinnamon and mix. Whisk the eggs in a large mixing bowl, then add the honey, milk, and salt. Slowly add your flour mixture to the wet ingredients, mixing as you pour. Once combined, add the strawberry chips. Pour the batter into the line pan and bake for 30 minutes. Because this is made with oat flour, don't expect it to rise as much as wheat flour does.

3. Remove from the oven and let the pan to cool on a wire rack before turning out the bread. Serve with strawberry jam (page 74).

How are other forms of life our creative partners?

Oats and peanuts work in partnership. Oats are annuals, undergoing the full cycle of life in one season. When legumes, such as peanut,s are harvested, they can leave an excess of nitrogen in the soil. Oats absorb the excess, use it for growth, and return it to the soil when tilled back into the ground once their grains are harvested, creating cyclical balance. For centuries, humans viewed oats only as food for beasts of burden. Even if that were true, where would we be today, were it not for oat-fueled horse power? The value of the food web extends far beyond what we choose to eat.

Savory Spinach and Mushroom Porridge

Now that we have embraced the wonders of oats, why not turn porridge on its head? Slower cooking, less processed, steel-cut oats can be prepared as a savory evening meal when you have more time. Try this one on a wintry evening.

Serves
4

Ingredients

2 tablespoons olive oil

1 onion, thinly sliced

1 teaspoon sugar

2 cups sliced cremini mushrooms

2 garlic cloves, minced

1 teaspoon paprika

1 cup steel-cut oats

5 tablespoons vermouth or dry white wine

2½ cups vegetable broth (page 108)

2 tablespoons butter or coconut oil

3½ cups baby spinach leaves

Sea salt

Method

1. Heat the oil in a large 9½-inch saucepan over medium heat. When hot, add the onion and sugar and cook for 5–7 minutes, until starting to soften. Add the mushrooms and cook for another 8 minutes. Add the garlic and paprika and mix in the oats, stirring to coat, then pour in the vermouth or wine. Let the oats absorb the wine, but no more than 30 seconds. Reduce the heat to low, add the broth, and cover the pan with a lid. Let cook for about 10 minutes, then remove the lid and stir it—all the broth should be absorbed.

2. Turn off the heat and add the butter or coconut oil, sea salt, and spinach. Cover and let sit for 3 minutes before serving.

> **Why do you consider certain foods to be breakfast foods?**
>
> There is power in how you decide to shape your meals. If nothing else, ask yourself a few questions about rules to which you hold fast. Why do you eat the way you do? Has it always been this way? Should it be different? If it were, what would that mean about how you exercise your values? Those questions are creation in action. Perhaps changing our meal culture could help to create a more regenerative food system?

German Onion Pie

I find it hard to imagine a world without onions. My partner, who hails from North Rhine-Westphalia, introduced Zwiebelkuchen (onion pie) into my life; it is now a lean-season tradition in our home. I serve it warm with a crisp white wine.

Serves
10

Ingredients
For the dough
½ (1-ounce) cake fresh yeast, or 2¼ teaspoons active dry yeast

Scant 1 cup warm water

2 teaspoons sugar

2 tablespoons olive oil

2 teaspoons salt

3¼ cups flour, plus extra for dusting

For the custard
5–6 large yellow onions (about 2¼ pounds)

3 tablespoons canola oil, plus extra for greasing

¾ cup heavy cream

3 eggs

1 teaspoon freshly grated nutmeg

2 teaspoons caraway seeds

Salt and pepper

Method

1. If using fresh yeast, crumble it into a bowl, add the water and sugar, and whisk until foamy. Add the olive oil and salt before gradually adding the flour, mixing as you do so. If using dry yeast, add all the dry ingredients to a bowl, mix well, then add the water and oil. Transfer to a floured surface and knead until you have a smooth dough, about 8 minutes. Put back into the bowl, cover with a dish towel, and let rise in a warm, dry place for 1 hour, until the dough has at least doubled in size.

2. Meanwhile, it's time for a good cry. Halve your onions and slice them vertically. Wearing glasses can help and choosing a milder variety, such a Spanish onion, will limit your tears.

3. Preheat the over to 400°F and grease a 16-inch square nonstick baking pan. Heat the oil in a large skillet and add the onions in handfuls. Stir as you go to coat the onions and prevent them sticking to the pan. Cook for 15–20 minutes until soft and golden. Make a custard by mixing the cream, eggs, nutmeg and salt and pepper.

4. Once your dough has risen, turn out onto a lightly floured surface. Knead for 5 minutes until it is elastic. Roll the dough into a rectangle roughly 2.5 cm/1 inch thick and place in the baking tray. Evenly distribute the onions over the dough and sprinkle with caraway seeds. Pour the custard over the top – you may need to tilt the tray to distribute it evenly. Bake for 25–30 minutes until the custard is set and the dough is golden.

What do our flavor preferences tell us about our evolution?

People have been eating onions for at least 7,000 years. Onions are full of water and offered our nomadic ancestors a source of hydration that was easily transported. Harvested late and stored in cool, dry cellars, or pickled or powdered, onions pack a sweet, flavorsome punch until a greater variety of foods make their appearance in the next growing season.

Preserved Pizza

Makes
4

Ingredients
For the dough

½ (1-ounce) cake fresh yeast, or 2¼ teaspoons active dry yeast

Scant 1 cup warm water

2 teaspoons sugar

2 tablespoons olive oil

2 teaspoons salt

3¼ cups flour, plus extra for dusting

2 tablespoons zero-waste tomato or carrot powder (pages 57 and 155) for added flavor (optional)

For the marinara sauce

2 (14½-ounce) cans of tomatoes

1 cup red wine

Salt

Pizza toppings

2 (4½-ounce) fresh mozzarella balls, sliced

Choice of vegetables (such as olives, bell peppers, tomatoes, mushrooms, onions, zucchini), thinly sliced

Basil leaves or pesto of your choice (pages 84–85)

Salt and pepper

Pizza, like risotto, offers a base for creativity, depending on the sauces and toppings you have on hand. This recipe incorporates many of the preserves in this book, so mix, match, and explore, adding toppings made from leftovers in the refrigerator.

Method

1. Prepare your dough following the method on page 95, adding some zero-waste tomato or carrot powder, if you prefer.

2. While the dough is rising, unless you have preserved tomato sauce (page 56) on hand, make a marinara sauce. Put the tomatoes, red wine, and a little salt into a saucepan, bring to a boil, then simmer for 40 minutes, until it thickens.

3. Preheat the oven to its hottest setting. Oil a baking sheet or two, or if you have a pizza stone, place it in the oven while you prepare your toppings.

4. Chop vegetables of your choice and consider adding dollops of any pesto you have prepped.

5. Flour a clean surface and a rolling pin. Divide your dough into four equal pieces and roll each one to a thickness of about ⅜ inch. Place the first piece of dough on a peel, if using a pizza stone, or an oiled baking sheet. Add a ladle or two of pizza sauce, spreading it with the back of a spoon. Top with the cheese and vegetables and put it in the oven for 5–10 minutes. Watch vigilantly to make sure the dough browns but doesn't burn to a crisp. Remove from the oven and repeat to make another three pizzas. Top with torn basil leaves or a few dollops of pesto before serving.

> **How can making pizza exercise your creativity?**
> Dough is alive and I love working with the life in my hands. When I think of it in that way, it becomes a nature-related practice for me, and the pizza becomes a collaborative creation between me, the yeast, the water, the flour, and the warm air that enables the dough to grow.

Purple Sauerkraut

Makes
About 4½ cups

Ingredients
1 medium head of red or green cabbage (about 2¼ pounds)
2 tablespoons kosher sea salt
1 tablespoon caraway seeds

How did preserves such as cabbage contribute to globalization?

Cabbage and creation go hand in hand. When humans discovered that lactobacillus converts the sugar in cabbage to lactic acid, preserves such as sauerkraut and kimchi were born. They enabled humans to do amazing things, including building the Great Wall of China all year round and circumnavigating the globe without developing scurvy. Fresh local cabbage is usually available in stores and markets throughout the winter. However, because I love the tang of sauerkraut, I take the time to make a small batch and to muse about how humans, cabbages, and bacteria toured the globe together and, for better or worse, they shaped our world. As you massage the leaves, focus on how the process makes visible our daily exchange with the invisible life that surrounds us.

Cabbage contains more vitamin C than citrus fruit and is easy to preserve, thanks to the life force that is lactobacillus bacteria. You can make sauerkraut with green cabbage, but it's equally good made with red. This recipe is designed to make one large jar—and to get you started playing with fermentation.

Method

1. Your tools here are: well-washed hands, a cutting board, a knife, a mixing bowl, a 2-quart pickling jar, a stone that just fits inside the jar, a clean dish towel, and a rubber band.

2. Preheat the oven to 350°F. Wash your jar and the stone, put into the oven for 10 minutes to sterilize, then remove and let cool.

3. Remove any outer layers of the cabbage that are starting to wilt and set aside. Quarter the cabbage, remove the tough core, then halve each quarter and cut those wedges into ribbonlike slices.

4. Transfer the chopped cabbage to a mixing bowl and use your hands to massage the cabbage with the salt for 10 minutes (the coarse salt crystals provide more surface area to absorb the water being drawn out of the cabbage). Consider how the color of your hands transforms as the cabbage does—a tangible exchange! Add the caraway seeds and mix. Pack the cabbage into the jar, making a fist to tamp it down. Pour any water extracted from the massage into the jar, cover with the limp outer leaves, and weigh it down with the stone. As fermentation begins, more water will be released from the cabbage. Cover the top of the jar with a clean dish towel secured with a rubber band to let air flow.

5. The following day, if the cabbage isn't covered in water, add 1 teaspoon of kosher salt to 1 cup of water and add what is needed to submerge the cabbage. While the sauerkraut ferments, keep it at room temperature (68°F) and away from direct sunlight. Keep an eye on your jar and you will notice bubbling bacteria in action. After three days, your sauerkraut will be ready to eat. It should last in the refrigerator for a couple of months.

Vegetarian Smørrebrød

Danish smørrebrød (meaning "buttered bread") is an open-style sandwich that makes a simple, irresistible meal. Keeping it midweek real, let's assume your bread is store bought. I use the almost black, large kernel rye bread popular in Nordic kitchens topped with a dash of cheddar and tangy sauerkraut and pickles.

Serves
4

Ingredients

4 slices of Nordic-style dark rye bread

Butter (page 156)

4 thick slices of vegetarian cheddar cheese

4 heaping tablespoons sauerkraut (page 100)

12 thinly sliced deli-style dill pickles or pickled pumpkin (pages 134 and 164)

1 apple, quartered, cored, and thinly sliced

Handful of cress or microgreens

Method

1. Preheat the broiler to medium hot.

2. Spread each slice of bread thickly with butter and place a hearty slice of cheddar on top. Add a layer of sauerkraut to each slice and place under the broiler for 4 minutes.

3. Layer 3 slices of the pickles and apples on top of each sandwich and sprinkle with cress or microgreens.

How do you express your identity in the food that you eat?

I have lived in Fairport (New York), Boston, Helsinki, London, and Copenhagen, and I identify with all those places. I see that blended identity in my food culture, a big part of which is the joy of preserved foods. All the ingredients in this recipe (including the bread and butter) can be considered preserves—creative inspirations that enabled people in all the towns I have called home to thrive in climates that are far from balmy for most of the year!

Wild Rice and Sauerkraut Salad

This dish pairs wild rice with that great lean-season preserve, sauerkraut, here made with green cabbage. Foraged wild rice is available, although most of what is in your supermarket will probably be cultivated, so the rice is far less wild than the name implies. However, I adore wild rice, because it reminds me that there is joy in going with the flow, letting nature take the lead and letting go of the need to control.

Serves

4

Ingredients

1 cup wild rice or a mixture of wild rice and basmati rice

3 tablespoons canola oil

1 onion, chopped

3 cups peeled and chopped celeriac (celery root; bite-size pieces)

1 tablespoon dried sage or marjoram

2 garlic cloves, minced

1 medium apple, cored and chopped

1¾ cups sauerkraut (page 100)

5 tablespoons apple cider vinegar

⅓ cup pumpkin seeds

Parsley leaves

Salt and pepper

Method

1. Fill a medium saucepan three-quarters full with water. Add a teaspoon of kosher salt and bring to a boil. Add the rice. Reduce the heat and follow the timing on the package for cooking the rice. Drain any remaining water from the pan.

2. Warm 1 tablespoon of the oil in a large skillet over medium heat. Add the onion and cook until softened, about 2 minutes. Add the celeriac and dried herbs and cook until softened, about 4 minutes. Toss in the garlic, apple, and sauerkraut, add a pinch of seasoning, and warm for 2 minutes before adding the rice to the pan. Turn off the heat and cover to keep warm.

3. Mix the rest of the oil and the vinegar in a small bowl with another pinch of seasoning. Transfer the rice and veggie mixture to a serving bowl. Add the dressing and the pumpkin seeds and give toss it. Sprinkle with parsley to serve.

How does our relationship with wild and domesticated foods differ?

Wild rice, as the name implies, was once produced not by the cultivated hand of humans, but by its own devices and relationships with the life-forms on which it depended. Humans let nature lead the way, and we foraged and harvested what we needed. Pause and consider the creative energy that was required to harvest and process wild rice.

Cabbage Chips

Who says that all chips need only be made of potatoes? They don't. The flavorful saltiness and crispy texture that makes potato chips so pleasing can be accomplished with plenty of other vegetables, such as the star of our lean-season kitchen—the cabbage. Any outer leaves you left out of your sauerkraut can be included here.

Serves
4–6

Ingredients
1 medium head of cabbage (about 2¼ pounds), or ½ head of red and ½ head of green cabbage
2 tablespoons olive oil
1 tablespoon paprika
Salt and pepper

Method
1. Preheat the oven to 350°F.

2. Tear each of the outer leaves of your cabbage coarsely into quarters, reserving the tougher leaves near the core for other recipes. Rinse the leaves, pat them completely dry, and toss them in a large mixing bowl with the oil, paprika, and a generous sprinkle of seasoning, making sure they are well coated.

3. Place a wire cooling rack on top of a baking sheet and lay the cabbage on top. Bake for 8–10 minutes, until crisp, then transfer to a wire rack, where they will continue to crisp up as they cool.

4. Serve as soon as possible as a snack, or add them to salads or sprinkle on top of pizzas or pasta dishes for some crunch.

What value is there in reworking traditional dishes?

When I make something new, my stimulated brain feels good. The process is often more important than the outcome. If the results are pleasing, I am proud. But, if they fall short, I often just find myself giggling and encouraged to try again. After all, when I question things I never bothered to before, I usually find value and pockets of joy lurking in places I never explored and that sets me thinking: What MORE can I learn?

Potato and Cabbage Patties

Known in the UK as bubble and squeak, this dish was invented to repurpose leftovers, so don't feel restricted by the recipe. If you don't have potatoes and cabbage, try it with carrots, Brussels sprouts, parsnips, squash, or celeriac (celery root).

Serves

As many as your leftovers allow—you want a volume ratio of 1:1

Ingredients

Leftover potatoes

Leftover cabbage

1 egg (optional)

2 tablespoons butter or coconut oil

Method

1. If your leftover potatoes or root vegetables were roasted, baked, or boiled, mash them but keep on the chunky side. Or, if the vegetables can be shredded, shred into thin slices, otherwise chop thinly. Mix your vegetables and potatoes together. Mix in an egg to bind, if needed.

2. Melt the butter or oil in a skillet over medium heat. Give yourself a mindful moment to listen to the fat bubbling in the pan.

3. Add your potato-and-vegetable mixture to form one large "cake" or separate the mixture into patties. Let "bubble and squeak" in the pan for 10 minutes—you want a nice brown crust to emerge on the bottom. The time it takes depends on how much butter or milk you used to make mashed potatoes in the first place. When you have a good brown crust, flip the cake or patties and fry on the other side for about 10 minutes.

4. Transfer from the pan to a plate lined with paper towels to soak up some of the fat. Serve as it is or with a dollop of applesauce (page 170), sauerkraut (page 100), or a fried egg.

> ### How do the sounds of cooking connect you to the elements?
> Bubble and Squeak is not merely a creative meal that avoids food waste, it is a mindful one that awakens all your senses. How often do we consider the well-being that comes from the sound of food? Cooking is a process of transformation that we nurture with the help of earth, wind, water, and fire. Bubbling, sizzling, crackling, and squeaking tune us into the presence of those elements in our kitchens.

Zero-waste Veggie Broth Box

In the lean-season recipes in this chapter, you have been peeling root vegetables and trimming off outer cabbage leaves and stems of broccoli and herbs, all of which can be repurposed. Find a large container and put it into your freezer. This is your broth box. Each time you find yourself with veg scraps on your cutting board, add them to the box. When it is full, make veggie broth to keep on hand for risotto (page 90), savory porridge (page 94), soup (page 110), or whatever else you can dream up. What was old is new again.

Ingredients

Vegetable peelings (including onion and garlic skins), outer leaves, and stems

Peppercorns

Bay leaves

Salt

Method

1. Make this when your freezer broth box is full to the brim, making sure that at least one-third of the contents are flavorful garlic and onion peelings.

2. Transfer your vegetables into a large stockpot and fill with water. You are aiming for a 1:1 ratio of water and vegetables by volume. Add a generous pinch of salt, some peppercorns and bay leaves, and bring to a boil. Once your broth boils, reduce the heat and simmer for 40 minutes. Strain the broth through a strainer and discard the vegetable parts. This time they are destined for your food waste bin, compost pile, or perhaps an animal looking for a tasty snack. You can use your broth immediately or store it in the freezer for up to three months.

> **Why do you label certain foods as waste? What would make you see waste differently?**
>
> As your nature-relatedness practice grows, every morsel of food will become more valuable to you, as they were for our ancestors. And as your desire to repurpose and reuse increases, you will hone your creative skills. That's how looking at things differently and asking new questions leads to new actions.

Stone Soup

Serves
6

Ingredients

2–3 tablespoons olive oil

2 yellow onions, finely chopped

5 garlic cloves, minced

A stone or pebble, sterilized in the oven at 350°F for 10 minutes

Stems of 3 heads of broccoli, peeled and chopped into ½-inch pieces, and a handful of florets, sliced

8–9 potatoes (about 2¼ pounds), cut into cubes

12½ cups vegetable broth (page 108)

Small handful of finely chopped flat-leaf parsley

Salt and pepper

Remember the story of Stone Soup? Once upon a time, a hungry traveler brings a stone to the door of an older woman and tells her he knows how to make the most delicious soup she has ever tasted. Intrigued, she puts the stone in a pot and adds water and meat. Word spreads and neighbors bring vegetables and beans. When everyone eats the soup together, it IS the most delicious soup they have ever tasted. The moral of the story is that we bring magical meaning to the ordinary when we work together as a community.

Method

1. Warm the oil in a large stockpot over medium heat and sauté the onions and garlic for 5 minutes until translucent. Add the stone and tell the tale of Stone Soup to whoever is in your kitchen. Ask them: Why do stones matter? What is the relationship between stones and water? What do stones add to soil to help us grow food? How do stones add value to our lives and our communities? How is food important for treating humans with dignity as well as nature? Keep cooking as you talk.

2. Add the broccoli stems, potatoes, broth, and seasoning. Bring to a boil, then simmer for 15 minutes. Add the broccoli florets and simmer for another 2 minutes. Sprinkle with the parsley and serve immediately with bread and homemade butter (page 156). Bring the stone to the table as decoration and keep it in the kitchen as a reminder to ask new questions about food, nature, and how you relate to it to build your nature-relatedness practice.

How does shifting the perspective on the story of eating bring new insights about your place in nature?

From a nature-relatedness perspective, I think the stone gets a rough deal in this story. After all, the stone helped to purify the water and add minerals to the soil to grow the vegetables and graze the animals. Would there be soup, or even a community of humans in that spot, were it not for the stones? This lean-season ritual aims to help you discover how widening the scope of your food stories builds your awareness of the nonhuman neighbors in your community and adds a dollop of extraordinary to an ordinary meal.

Eating
for
Connection

Cultivating your Identity as Nature

To be human is to be social. The deeper your connections to others, the more you identify with them and feel validated and safe. When your social connections break down, you feel anxious. Where does the rest of nature fit into this? Americans and the redwoods, the British and their White Cliffs, your family and that special tree in the park . . . nature is a part of your social identity.

Developing a nature-relatedness practice deepens your sense of identity as a part of your habitat. As you progress, you begin to derive well-being benefits and behave in a more collaborative way with all the life that makes up your community. The Pulitzer Prize-winning Harvard evolutionary biologist E. O. Wilson explained in *Biophilia*:

"It is possible to spend a lifetime in a Magellanic voyage around the trunk of a single tree. [As] the exploration is pressed, it will engage more the things close to the human heart and spirit . . . humanity is exalted not because we are so far above other living creatures, but because knowing them well elevates the very concept of life."

Each plate of food you eat presents an opportunity for a Magellan-like journey, even for people in urban jungles, because eating is an exchange with the rest of the natural world—the life that produced your food, the bacteria that lives in your body to break down the nutrients you must absorb, and the life you foster when you burn the energy you consumed. And much of the life you are in exchange with resides under your feet.

Eating: An Act of Exchange
Ninety-five percent of our food grows in soil, one teaspoon of which can contain more life than there are humans on the earth (7.5 billion). Just like every human, the life that makes soil fertile needs water, energy, and carbon. Buried plant matter, decomposed and compressed over millennia, and containing the energy from photosynthesis, becomes the carbon-rich fossil fuels that we extract from the ground. Just as fossil fuels are finite, so too is soil. When soil is stressed by monocropping (continuously farming a single crop and excluding other plants), biodiversity loss, and forest degradation, eventually the soil will fail. It takes 1,000 years to generate about an inch of topsoil, and according to the United Nations, the soil we need to grow food will be eliminated in a few decades if we don't reverse the current rate of degradation.

The International Panel on Climate Change (IPCC) has reported that 89 percent of all agricultural emissions can be mitigated by improving carbon levels in our soil. (Carbon itself is not bad, it is one of the foundations of life for all living things. By valuing carbon's place in the life cycle, we begin to value the natural role of soil, wetlands, and trees for capturing carbon and removing it from the atmosphere to improve the conditions for people and the rest of life on the planet.) That means that eating to promote a regenerative food system is more complicated than adopting a plant-based diet. Eating to promote a regenerative system requires consideration of how every foodstuff you eat is produced in relationship to the health of the overall ecosystem.

Supporting farmers, politicians, and companies who focus on agroecology helps to make regenerative agriculture a social priority. On a personal level, committing to eat in tune with the seasons and buying from regional producers that have a diverse yield will help you to do research to understand the issues in your local community. These farms will probably produce a smaller yield of each crop than a monocropping system, but often a larger overall yield (with far less chemical input), because they nurture a balanced, regenerative food system instead of trying to control a plot of land. Such farming systems often incorporate domesticated animals reared with the same respect as the family pet, because they play important roles in the ecosystem in the form of supplying natural fertilization and weed control.

Questioning what it takes to put food on your plate is also good practice. It expands your knowledge of how intimately connected all of life is. Along the way, you experience how relating to nature can elevate Wilson's "very concept of life."

> ## Humanity is exalted not because we are so far above other living creatures, but because knowing them well elevates the very concept of life

Ritual

**Rituals with Nature
for Connection:
For the Birds**

As the year shifts seasons, the population of birds that surround you shift, too. When you rise in the morning, open a window and listen for a minute. What do you hear? Are there times of year when you hear more birdsong than others? We know many birds are migratory, flying to warmer climes during winter and returning to their breeding grounds in spring. In Europe, for example, the ritual of Valentine's Day originally marked the time of year between the winter solstice and the spring equinox when migratory birds returned, and love was once again literally in the air as those busy pollinators made the world fertile once again. Does the weather impact on the songs of your feathered friends? Birds are great bellwethers that can tune us into the changing seasons, growing patterns, and even the impacts of climate change. Lean in, listen, and routinely connect with the story the birds are trying to tell. Does it match your own?

Ritual

**Rituals with Food
for Connection:
Nature's New Year**

Our January ritual of making New Year's resolutions was originally practiced at the vernal equinox more than 4,000 years ago. It was in spring as ancient Babylonians readied to sow their seed that they resolved to return tools, pay off debts, and generally be better people to appease the gods and ensure a robust harvest.

I don't go in for cold turkey New Year's resolutions, because I think enduring change happens gradually. However, I am inspired by our agricultural ancestors to set intentions to build a nature-related practice with food at nature's new year in spring, when the earth renews itself, as opposed to the beginning of the calendar year. The ritual recipes offered in this chapter are designed for you to heighten your connection with the reawakening of life throughout the spring, as you develop your nature-relatedness practice from head to hands to habit.

Cheddar and Ale Rarebit

Here is a dish to make in early spring with what remains of the winter pantry. The ingredients are all preserves from the harvest: the flour, the beer, and, of course, cheese is "preserved" milk.

Method

1. Preheat the broiler to medium heat. Melt the butter in a saucepan, add the flour, and stir constantly for 2–3 minutes to make a roux, then keep stirring as you pour in the beer. Remove from the heat and mix in the mustard, horseradish, and Worcestershire sauce. Return the pan to low heat, add the cheese, and mix until melted.

2. Toast your bread under the broiler on both sides. Remove, place on a baking sheet, and spoon the cheese mixture over each slice. Sprinkle with a few more drops of Worcestershire sauce and broil for 3–4 minutes, until the cheese is golden and bubbling.

Serves
4

Ingredients
3½ tablespoons butter
3 tablespoons all-purpose flour
⅔ cup stout or dark ale
1 teaspoon whole-grain mustard
1 teaspoon grated horseradish
1 teaspoon Worcestershire sauce
1¾ cup shredded vegetarian aged cheddar cheese
4 thick slices of sourdough bread

Why don't we consider all foods to be rare-bits?

How this traditional dish from Wales earned its name is unknown but the consensus is that "rarebit" is a corruption of the word "rabbit." How fitting for a meal that was served when winter grudgingly gave way to spring, rabbits being an age-old symbol of spring fertility. I suspect all food seemed like "rare" bits to our ancestors.

Leek and Carrot Coconut Soup

Leeks are a hardy plant that can thrive at subzero temperatures. In season from fall to late spring, they remind us that life always finds a way, even in the harshest conditions. Leeks make a hearty soup, enriched by the coconut milk, but you could always omit it and add more broth for a less creamy version.

Serves
6–8

Ingredients

3 tablespoons coconut oil

6 large carrots, peeled and chopped (save the peels for zero-waste carrot powder, page 155)

1 large onion, chopped

2 leeks, halved lengthwise, then chopped

3 garlic cloves, minced

1 tablespoon grated fresh ginger

4¼ cups vegetable broth (page 108)

1¾ cups coconut milk

2 fresh thyme sprigs

Salt and pepper

Method

1. Melt 1 tablespoon of the coconut oil in a stockpot over a medium heat before adding the carrots, onion, leeks, garlic, and ginger. Cook for 5 minutes, until softened. Add the broth and coconut milk, bring to a boil, and simmer for 25 minutes.

2. When you have finished your daydreaming, your soup will be ready to serve, either as it is, chunky, or use a handheld immersion blender if you prefer it smooth.

3. If you want, mix some carrot powder (page 155) with a pinch of salt, pepper, and a few thyme leaves and sprinkle over each bowl before serving.

> **How is your resilience interconnected with that of the rest of life on the earth?**
>
> Legend has it that Saint David advised troops in Wales to pin leeks to their caps in battle to differentiate them from the enemy. Now the national emblem of Wales, leeks became a symbol of resilience, an example of humans reflecting qualities they observe in nature.

Mint and Cilantro Chutney

I like to mix up this vibrant-green mint and cilantro chutney to use on bread, yogurt, or with veggies as a dip for crudités and to breathe in my connection with my surroundings as spring sets in.

Makes
About ½ cup

Ingredients
2 garlic cloves, minced
1 tablespoon finely grated fresh ginger
1 teaspoon sugar
¼ teaspoon salt
1 cup finely chopped mint leaves
2 cups finely chopped cilantro, leaves and stems
1 teaspoon apple cider vinegar
1 tablespoon water

Optional
Yogurt
Fresh chile, chopped

Method
1. Grind the garlic, ginger, sugar, and salt in a food processor until coarsely chopped. If you have time, you can also do this using a mortar and pestle. Add the mint and cilantro, a handful at a time. Drizzle in the vinegar and water, and continue to grind to a coarse but creamy consistency.

2. If you want to make the chutney creamier, add 3–4 tablespoons of yogurt to the mix. Or, if you want to make it a little spicy, add a fresh chile to the mix.

What does spring fever feel like?

Nature-related practices nurture feelings of interconnectedness with all forms of life. Think about your connection with mint. Can you imagine your life without it? Mint feels fresh in winter and zingy in spring. From toothpaste to chewing gum to tea, many of us use mint daily to heighten our senses. Mint isn't just pleasurable, it gives clarity, making us more aware of ourselves and our surroundings.

Chutney-marinated Halloumi Salad

I love the rubbery texture of halloumi, because it makes me slow down and savor the cheese itself. The salt brining process used to preserve the cheese results in its firm texture, which lends itself perfectly to being broiled, fried, or barbecued.

Serves
4

Ingredients

1 pound halloumi, sliced

¼ cup mint and cilantro chutney (see recipe facing page)

2 tablespoons olive oil, plus extra for broiling

2 onions, sliced in rings

2 heads of mini romaine lettuce, or other lettuce, washed and chopped

1 tablespoon apple cider vinegar

Salt and pepper

Method

1. Put the halloumi into a bowl, add the mint chutney and 1 tablespoon of the olive oil, and stir to coat the halloumi. Cover and marinate for 30 minutes.

2. Warm a skillet with a small splash of olive oil, put the onion rings into the pan, and sauté for 4 minutes, until softened. Push them to the side and place the halloumi in the pan, evenly spaced. Fry on each side for 1–2 minutes, until brown. Remove from the heat.

3. Toss the lettuce with the chutney used for the marinade and add another tablespoon of olive oil and the vinegar. Place your lettuce on serving dishes and top with the warm onions and halloumi. Add a grinding of pepper and some salt of the earth.

Why do we say "the salt of the earth"?

Where does salt come from? The sea. So, when I eat this simple spring salad, I pause and remind myself of the oceans of our blue planet from which the flavor of life literally comes. Salt was once considered so valuable it is the origin for the word "salary." Chew over the value of small details we often take for granted when whipping up this tasty recipe.

Spring Pea, Mint, and Feta Frittata

Peas, feta, and eggs are a delicious combination for a tasty lunch or light dinner. Pep this up with some of the mint and cilantro chutney and mint leaves to bring a fresh focus to your life.

Serves
4

Ingredients

1 tablespoon olive oil

1 onion, chopped

2 garlic cloves, minced

4 eggs

2 tablespoons milk

1 teaspoon Dijon mustard

½ teaspoon smoked paprika

½ teaspoon salt

1 cup peas (fresh or frozen)

⅓ cup crumbled feta cheese

4 teaspoons mint and cilantro chutney (page 118)

Fresh mint leaves, to serve

Method

1. Preheat the oven to 350°F. Warm the olive oil in an ovenproof skillet over low heat, add the onion and garlic, and sauté for 2 minutes. Meanwhile, whisk the eggs, milk, and mustard together. Stir the smoked paprika, salt, and peas into the egg mixture.

2. Remove the pan from the heat and pour in the egg mixture. Place the pan in the oven and cook for 10 minutes, until it settles. Remove and sprinkle the crumbled feta cheese on top. Return to the oven for 1 minute to let it soften.

3. Remove from the oven, top with four dollops of mint chutney and sprinkle with fresh mint. Serve warm, straight from the pan.

How might your view of the world be different if the vernal equinox marked your New Year?

Historically, the vernal (spring) equinox marked the beginning of the New Year. Julius Caesar created the month of January, but new-year celebrations only shifted to winter when the clock was invented and we began to shape time ourselves as opposed to aligning our actions with nature's timepiece, the sun. When the vernal equinox arrives and day becomes equal to night, I pause and consider how I might live my life differently if I aligned my clock with Mother Nature's. Something to ponder as you make this frittata.

Split Pea Burgers

Try these burgers when you're feeding a crowd—they're great
served with mint chutney (page 118), sauerkraut (page 100), or
a piece of mint-marinated fried halloumi (page 119).

Makes
8

Ingredients

1 tablespoon olive oil

1 cup finely chopped red onion

1½ cups shredded carrot (or
zucchini, or finely chopped
bell pepper, or whatever is
on hand and seasonal)

1 garlic clove, minced

1¾ cups finely chopped
mushrooms

3 cups vegetable broth
(page 108)

1 cup dried split peas

½ cup brown rice

1 teaspoon ground coriander

1 teaspoon ground cumin

½ cup dried bread crumbs

3 tablespoons olive oil
(optional)

Salt and pepper

Method

1. Heat the olive oil in a medium saucepan. Add the onion
and carrot and sauté over medium-low heat with a pinch of
salt for 5–7 minutes. Add the garlic and mushrooms and sauté
for 4 minutes. Add the vegetable broth, split peas, brown rice,
coriander, and cumin. Bring to a boil, reduce the heat, and let
simmer for 1 hour, until the peas have been rehydrated. Remove
from the heat and let the mix cool for 5 minutes.

2. Working in batches, put the mixture into a blender, one ladleful
at a time. Pulse each batch a few times; do not puree. The texture
needs to be smooth but still retain some chunkiness. Remove each
batch to a mixing bowl before pulsing the next batch. Add the
bread crumbs to the bowl and season. Refrigerate for 30 minutes.

3. Preheat the broiler to medium hot. Alternatively, heat half
the olive oil in a skillet. Use your hands to shape the mixture into
8 patties and then broil or, working in batches, fry for 4 minutes,
flip, and cook the other side. Use the remaining oil to fry the second
batch. Serve immediately.

How is your life connected with the life in fertile soil?

Mars, best known as the god of war, is also the god of agriculture. In Roman
times, the last breath of winter gave way to the first breath of battle as
sun, warmth, and food made warfare possible. Mars battled the enemy and
the elements, helping to ensure victory on the farmer's field as well as the
campaign. The two were connected. I like to make these split pea burgers and
muse about the less-considered connections in my life.

Leek and Hazelnut Risotto

Risotto is one of those dishes that cannot be rushed. It is hard not to feel connected to your food as you stand and stir it for 20 minutes. To make this cooking moment a nature-related one, set an intent before you begin to consider a New Year resolution as you stir. What can you do to develop your understanding of the way all the food you eat connects you to the wider ecosystem?

Serves

4

Ingredients

1 cup chopped hazelnuts

2 tablespoons olive oil, plus extra for drizzling

2 small onions, finely chopped

2 celery stalks, thinly sliced

3 garlic cloves, minced

4 leeks (about 1 pound), sliced lengthwise and chopped

1⅓ cups risotto rice

Scant 1 cup vermouth or dry white wine

2¾ cups hot vegetable broth (page 108)

Method

1. Preheat the oven to 300°F. Spread the chopped hazelnuts on a baking sheet and roast for 10 minutes or until browned. Remove from the oven and place a cloth over them to keep them warm.

2. Heat the olive oil in a medium saucepan. Add the onion and celery and soften for 2 minutes over low heat. Add the garlic and soften for 2 minutes before adding the leeks. After a minute, add the rice. Quickly pour in the vermouth or dry white wine and let the rice absorb the wine as the liquid reduces. Spoon in the hot broth, one ladle at a time, and stir until each ladle of broth has been absorbed before adding the next. Repeat until all the broth has been absorbed, which takes 15–20 minutes, and taste the rice to make sure it is tender but chewy.

3. Turn off the heat and add the hazelnuts and another drizzle of olive oil. Cover and let sit for 2–3 minutes before serving so that the rice absorbs all the flavors.

> **How do you resolve to be more connected with nature in the "new year"?**
>
> View your nature-related resolutions (perhaps becoming a more plant-based eater, a less consumptive shopper, a muscle-power or a public-transport devotee) as long-term goals. Then make a plan that focuses on how to build intent, awareness, new knowledge, and the connections you need to have experiences that help you build a culture and community that better mirrors nature.

Cannellini Beans, Ale, Mustard, and Truffle Stew

This dish is one of my absolute favorite winter into spring meals. Beans are summer crops, but because they dry and preserve well, they remain a staple source of protein in my kitchen throughout the months, when fresh foods are few and far between.

Serves
4

Ingredients

1¼ cups dried cannellini beans

1 teaspoon baking soda

1 tablespoon canola oil

1 medium onion, diced

6 garlic cloves, minced

1½ cups dark or ruby ale

2 cups vegetable broth (page 108)

3 tablespoons honey or apple molasses (page 171)

3 dried bay leaves

3 rosemary sprigs

¼ cup apple cider vinegar

¼ cup whole-grain mustard, mild to medium heat

2 teaspoons truffle oil

Salt and pepper

Method

1. Put the cannellini beans into a bowl, cover them with water (with room to spare), and let soak overnight.

2. The following day, remove any loose skins. Rinse the beans thoroughly. Put into a saucepan, cover with water, and add the baking soda. Bring to a boil, cook for 10 minutes, and skim off any skins that rise to the surface. After 10 minutes, reduce the heat and simmer for 1 hour. Drain.

3. Warm the oil in a large saucepan, add the onion, and sauté for 2 minutes, then add the garlic and cook for 1 minute before stirring in the drained beans. Pour in the ale, stock, honey or molasses, and herbs. Bring to a boil and simmer for 30 minutes.

4. Add the vinegar, mustard, and seasoning and simmer for another 30 minutes–1 hour, depending on taste and how quickly your beans are cooking. If you have any frozen vegetables, add a few handfuls to the stew for some extra color.

5. Remove the herbs, strip the rosemary needles from the sprigs, and chop. Transfer the beans to a serving bowl and sprinkle the rosemary on top. Drizzle the truffle oil over the beans and serve.

How instinctual are your eating choices?

Humans are not the only creatures to rely on beans for protein. Deer, rabbits, and chipmunks are ones that share our taste, a reminder that our diet is shaped by instinct and intellect. Our brains would not have evolved as they have without nutritious food and the need to develop memory and rationality to recall what to eat, where to find it, and how to cook it. Developing a diet that nourishes people and planet requires a balance of instinct and intellect. To kindle both, this spring dish relies on preserves. A seasonal diet mirrors the fact that spring is a time for growth, not abundant harvest.

Rhubarb-marinated Tofu Steaks

Here is a meatless barbecue recipe that highlights one of the most robust vegetables to be harvested in spring, rhubarb. It marries well with spices and soy sauce to make a suitably tangy marinade.

Serves
4

Ingredients
1¼ pounds firm tofu

For the marinade
1 tablespoon olive oil
1 small onion, chopped
2 garlic cloves, minced
3 large rhubarb stalks, chopped
¼ cup ketchup
2 tablespoons water
1 tablespoon apple molasses (page 171) or maple syrup
2 teaspoons whole-grain mustard
1 tablespoon soy sauce
1 teaspoon cumin

Method
1. Cut your tofu into 8 chunky slices, about ⅝ inch thick. Set aside.

2. Warm the olive oil in a skillet, add the onion, and sauté over medium heat for 3 minutes, until softened. Add the garlic and sauté for 1 minute. Add the rhubarb along with the rest of the marinade ingredients. Bring the mixture to a boil, then simmer for 15 minutes. After the rhubarb has softened, let the mixture cool slightly, then blend to the consistency of a sauce and cool.

3. Coat the tofu steaks with the sauce and marinate for at least 30 minutes. The longer the marinating time, the more flavor soaks into the steaks. Gently warm the steaks in the marinade until heated through.

4. Alternatively, heat a heavy skillet or a cast-iron griddle pan and grill the steaks for a minute or two on each side, gently warm the remaining sauce, and pour it over the steaks.

> **How can seasonal eating create balance between vulnerability and resilience?**
>
> The vernal equinox is a time of balance. Day and night are of equal length. All life on the planet is experiencing a rebalancing. New life begins to find its roots, tentatively flourishing toward an unknown future. Seasonal eating shifts your experience of life to one that is more harmonious with your habitat. As the foods of spring appear, ask yourself how balanced is your life with the life on which you depend?

Rhubarb and Lentil Curry

In 1837, a variety of rhubarb was created in England in honor of Queen Victoria's coronation. "Victoria" rhubarb is still prized by gardeners. What kind of rhubarb did you find in the market?

Method

1. Put 2 cups of water and the rice into a large saucepan. Bring to a boil, then reduce the heat, cover, and simmer for 25 minutes, or according to package directions, until all the water has been absorbed.

2. Meanwhile, heat the oil in a skillet, add the onion, and sauté for 2 minutes, then add the garlic and cook for 1 minute before mixing in the ginger and spice. Cook for 2 minutes to release the aromas before adding the lentils and ⅔ cup boiling water, stirring until the water is absorbed. Add the rhubarb, honey, and another ⅔ cup boiling water. Cook for 10 minutes, stirring occasionally, until tender. Stir in the spinach—it will wilt as you combine.

3. Fluff up your rice, transfer to a serving platter, top with the lentils, and serve dolloped with mint chutney.

Serves
4

Ingredients

1 cup brown basmati rice or other long-grain rice

1 tablespoon olive oil

1 onion, chopped

1 garlic clove, minced

2 teaspoons grated fresh ginger

2 teaspoons garam masala

1 teaspoon ground turmeric

¾ cup lentils (use what is on hand and check whether they need presoaking)

2 large stalks rhubarb (about 1 pound), chopped into bite-size pieces

1 tablespoon honey

2 handfuls of fresh spinach leaves

Mint and cilantro chutney (page 118), to serve

Why do we celebrate human diversity but opt for conformism with much of the natural world?

There are 250,000 known edible plant species. Today, 75 percent of our food comes from just twelve of them. How boring. How dangerous. Our desire for uniform monocrops is destroying ecosystem biodiversity: the insects, birds, bacteria, and worms that perpetuate the cycle of life. Learning the difference between varieties of common foods helps us connect with biodiversity.

New Potato Salad

In my part of the world, it is hard to miss the excitement when Jersey Royals arrive. Whichever new potato is common in your neck of the woods, pay attention to the timing of its arrival. Persistent spring rains and frost will postpone and lighten the harvest. Serve this seasonal side with the split pea burgers (page 122), halloumi salad (page 119), pea frittata (page 120), or tofu steak (page 127).

Serves
6–8 as a side

Ingredients
2¼ pounds Jersey Royals or any local new potato variety

⅔ cup olive oil

⅔ cup red wine vinegar

1 bunch of fresh soft herbs (such as chervil, mint, parsley, or lovage), coarsely chopped

1 red or white onion, thinly sliced

1⅓ cups chopped cornichons

Salt and pepper

Method

1. Wash the potatoes and put them whole into a pan with enough salted cold water to cover the potatoes by at least 1½ inches. Bring to a boil and cook for 5–10 minutes. Drain and transfer to a board.

2. Using a cloth to protect your hand from the heat, gently smash the boiled potatoes so that they split apart (this will help the oil and vinegar to penetrate the skins). Transfer the potatoes to a bowl and add the oil and vinegar while they are still warm. Stir to evenly coat the potatoes, then mix in the herbs, onion, and cornichons. Season with salt and pepper.

Why do we feel a connection with new potatoes, unlike others?

In Elizabethan England, when potatoes from exotic lands reached the court, they were considered aphrodisiacs. Paradoxically, the potato's reproductive power soon relegated it to peasant food status. From fries to mashed potatoes, our love of potatoes has long since been revived. Yet, it is a love we take for granted—until spring, when the first flavorful "apples of the earth" appear.

Asparagus Salad

The asparagus season is special. When the stalks shoot up from the ground in late spring, asparagus regally adorns menus—as any vegetable with a crown should.

Serves
4 as a side

Ingredients
1 bunch of green asparagus
⅔ cup olive oil
¼ cup balsamic vinegar
Salt and pepper

Method
1. Prepare the asparagus for steaming by chopping off the woody ends; the stalks will naturally snap where the tender part starts.

2. Boil some water in a shallow saucepan and blanch the asparagus (2–3 minutes for skinnier spears, 4–5 minutes for thicker ones). Drain and lay on a cutting board to cool. Chop the asparagus into thirds and toss with the olive oil and balsamic vinegar. Season and serve.

How can we value all foods as much as we do asparagus?

Throughout its history, the arrival of new-season asparagus has been greeted with a fanfare of joy and relish. Perhaps precisely because its season is so short, we see the benefit of seasonally eating asparagus more than other plants.

Radishes à la française

This simple French dish of crunchy radishes, butter, and salt was enjoyed by market porters in Paris as a midmorning snack. Eating it reminds me that every bite I take is taking a bite out of life.

Serves
4 as a snack

Ingredients
1 large bunch of radishes, preferably a variety with a plump firm bulb

½ cup plus 3 tablespoons (5½ ounces) butter (page 156), softened

3 tablespoons sea salt

Method

1. Wash and dry the radishes and remove the tips that are connected to the roots so that they have a flat bottom. If there are still leafy tops on the radishes, remove the leaves and reserve them for use in a salad.

2. Dip each radish in butter, then brush with salt before eating.

How does your outlook on life change when spring arrives?

Radishes do not have the rock-star status of asparagus. Yet, rewind the clocks and imagine how the peppery snap of a radish must have tasted to humans anxious about the success of the new growing season. Not to mention, finally, some fresh food!

Deli-style Dill Pickles

Makes
2 jars

Ingredients
12 small pickling cucumbers,
about 4 inches long
⅓ quantity pickling spice
(see below)
6 garlic cloves, halved
2 fresh dill feathery leaves or
use 1 tablespoon dried dill
5½ cups water
1 cup white vinegar
⅔ cup kosher salt

For the pickling spice
2 tablespoons mustard seeds
1 tablespoon juniper seeds
2 teaspoons coriander seeds
1 heaping teaspoon crushed
red pepper flakes
1 teaspoon ground ginger
3 bay leaves, crumbled
2 cinnamon sticks, crumbled
6 whole cloves

As spring gives way to summer, what do you intend to preserve about your heightened sense of connection to the rest of the natural world since the rebalancing moment of the vernal equinox? Take an afternoon in late spring to consider the question as you transform cucumbers into pickles, creating a crunch for more consideration of connection later in the year.

Method

1. First make the pickling spice by combining all the spices. This amount makes enough to use for three recipes. Use one-third for this recipe; store the rest in a sealed jar for several months.

2. Wash the cucumbers (halve or quarter them if they are chunky) and pack them upright into sterilized jars (see page 60 for how to sterilize the jars). Evenly divide half the spice mix between the jars; do the same with half the garlic and half the dill.

3. Combine the water, vinegar, and salt in a large bowl, stirring until the salt dissolves, add the remaining spice mix, garlic, and dill, then pour over the pickles to submerge. Let the jars stand at room temperature for 24 hours with the lids slightly open. After 24 hours, taste and add more vinegar, if you want.

4. If you want to keep the pickles for many months, process them following the method on page 60, or seal the jar and store in the refrigerator for three days and eat within a week or two.

A cucumber is 95 percent water. About 60 percent of your body is water. You have to drink water; you don't produce it and that exchange facilitates more exchange with the natural world. Water is critical to enable you to absorb minerals and nutrients from food, to facilitate your organ functions, and to remove toxins from your body. Making pickles is a tangible reminder of exchange as you watch the salt and sugar draw water from the cucumbers to create this refreshing summer snack.

Baby Broccoli, Chickpeas, and Tahini

Seasonal leafy veggies adds a colorful crunch to a warm salad with a tahini dressing. Eating early spring's baby broccoli in season is one way to align ourselves with the phases of nature.

Serves
2 as a main, 4 as a side

Ingredients
8 ounces baby broccoli

2 tablespoons olive oil

1 (15-ounce) can of chickpeas (garbanzo beans), rinsed and drained

1 teaspoon crushed red pepper flakes

Small bunch of radishes, thinly sliced and green parts (if included) chopped

For the dressing
¼ cup tahini (page 25)

2 tablespoons apple cider vinegar

1 teaspoon honey

1 garlic clove, minced

1 tablespoon extra virgin olive oil

2 teaspoons sunflower seeds

Method

1. First make the dressing by whisking together the tahini, vinegar, honey, garlic, and a pinch of salt. Add a tablespoon of water, if the tahini needs cutting, to become runny. Whisk in the extra virgin olive oil. Mix in the seeds.

2. Bring a large saucepan of salted water to a boil. Chop the woody ends off the baby broccoli and slice the stems lengthwise. Boil for 3–4 minutes, until just tender, drain, and rinse with cold water. Spread on a clean dish towel to dry the leaves.

3. Preheat the broiler. Warm 1 tablespoon of oil in a skillet, add the chickpeas, and red pepper flakes, and stir-fry for 3–4 minutes, until warm. Toss the broccoli in another tablespoon of oil and put under the broiler for 1–2 minutes, until lightly charred. Turn off the heat for the chickpeas, add the broccoli to the pan, and mix. Transfer to a serving bowl, add the radishes, and toss with the dressing.

How would the pace of your life differ if you aligned time with the earth's orbit around the sun?

In sixteenth-century France, Charles IX tried to move the agricultural new year in spring to the calendrical new year in winter. Rural folk protested, and farmers couldn't fathom celebrating new year in dormant winter. City dwellers saw this as backward thinking: Why should human progress be subject to nature? Have we have come full circle in our thinking?

Roasted Carrot Couscous

Roasting transforms spring carrots, making them all the sweeter, and turning a simple couscous into a complete meal.

Serves
4

Ingredients

6 carrots, peeled and cut into bite-size pieces (reserve peels to make zero-waste carrot powder, page 155)

¼ cup olive oil

1⅓ cups couscous

Rind of a quarter of preserved lemon (page 38), optional

1½ cups hot vegetable broth (page 108)

1 small onion, chopped

2 garlic cloves, minced

¼ cup chopped walnuts

½ teaspoon chili powder

1 teaspoon cumin

Salt and pepper

Torn parsley or cilantro leaves, to serve

Method

1. Preheat the oven to 400°F.

2. Put the carrots onto a large baking sheet and toss to coat in 2 tablespoons of olive oil. Season and roast for 15–20 minutes, until tender.

3. Put the couscous into a bowl, add a tablespoon of oil and the preserved lemon (if using), and mix. Pour the hot broth over the couscous. Cover with a clean dish towel and rest for 10 minutes.

4. Heat another tablespoon of the oil in a skillet, add the onion and garlic, and sauté for 2 minutes before adding the walnuts, chili powder, and cumin. Cook for another 2 minutes. Fluff your couscous and lay on a serving platter, top with roasted carrots, and sprinkle with the onion-and-nut mixture. Add fresh herbs and serve.

> **How does cooking help you to understand that you are in constant exchange with the rest of the natural world?**
>
> Each day 7 percent of your body mass is exchanged as you breathe, eat, drink, and move. What you are at the start of the day is not what you are at the end of it. Why? Because nature is not OUT there, it is IN you. When I cook and see other life transformed in heat, water, and contact with other elements, it helps me to visualize how my body is constantly changing in exchange with all the visible and invisible elements of my environment.

Carrot Gnocchi

Homemade gnocchi are comfort food at its best. I like to make them with carrots instead of the traditional all-potato version.

Serves
4

Ingredients
2 large baking potatoes (about 1 pound)

3 medium carrots (about 6 ounces), peeled (save the skins to make carrot powder, page 155) and thinly sliced

1 egg, beaten

1 teaspoon salt

1¾ cups "00" Italian pasta flour or cake flour or 1⅔ cups all-purpose flour, plus extra as needed

Salt and pepper

To serve
Preserved tomato sauce (page 56) or pesto (pages 84–85)

or

¼ cup olive oil

1 garlic clove, minced

Handful of chopped sage

Method

1. Preheat the oven to 400°F. Pierce the skins of the potatoes a few times and bake for about 1 hour, until soft. Toward the end of the cooking time, drop the carrots into a saucepan of boiling water and boil until soft, about 15 minutes. Drain thoroughly, then puree in a food processor. Halve the potatoes, scoop out the flesh, and push through a potato ricer. Transfer the pureed carrots and potato into a bowl, add the egg, and salt and mix.

2. Gradually add the flour, about 2 heaping tablespoons at a time, kneading to form a dough that is stiff but still a little sticky. Tear off a small piece and drop into boiling water. If it holds its shape, the dough is ready. If not, add more flour and test another piece. Once you're happy with it, cut the dough into four pieces.

3. Flour a work surface and roll each piece into a ¾-inch-thick log. Use a knife to cut into bite-size lengths that resemble pillows. Keep them they are, or press your thumb into the center of each one, bring in the sides, then roll each one against the tines of a fork to create ridges. Put onto a baking sheet lined with parchment paper.

4. Fill a large saucepan with salted water and bring to a boil. Add the gnocchi, a handful at a time, and cook for 4–5 minutes, until they float to the top and are firm. Use a slotted spoon to transfer them to a wire rack and cover with a dish towel to keep warm while you cook the rest.

5. To serve, gently warm the tomato sauce or pesto. Alternatively, heat the olive oil in a skillet and add the garlic, sage, and seasoning. Remove your chosen sauce from the heat after 3–4 minutes, coat the gnocchi, and toss before serving.

> **What is the difference between humans forcing and nurturing nature?**
> Although we associate carrots with spring, the carrot season usually doesn't come until early summer, weather dependent. So why are local carrots often available any time of the year? As colder days set in, farmers lay blankets of straw on top of their carrot crops to warm the soil system, making year-round harvest possible. Is that forcing or nurturing nature?

Sweet
Rhubarb Pie

I love baking pies to share with friends and, as I do, I lend a thought to what secrets the plant that provided my filling shared with me. This one is all rhubarb but, when strawberry season arrives, I mix strawberries and rhubarb together for a delicious combination. A little vinegar in the dough gives a tang to the buttery pastry, a flavor I recall from my childhood days.

Serves

8

Ingredients

For the dough

2⅔ cups organic all-purpose flour, plus extra for dusting

2 tablespoons sugar

¾ cup (6 ounces) butter (page 156)

1 egg

2 teaspoons white wine vinegar

¼ cup ice-cold water

Salt

For the filling

2½ pounds rhubarb, chopped

1½ cups sugar

1 tablespoon all-purpose flour

½ teaspoon ground cinnamon

1 teaspoon vanilla extract or vanilla sugar

4 tablespoons butter

Method

1. Preheat the oven to 375°F and lightly grease a 9 x 7-inch pie dish.

2. Put the flour, sugar, butter, and a pinch of salt into a bowl and blend by crisscrossing two knives, or rub in with your fingertips until the mixture resembles fine bread crumbs. In a separate bowl, whisk the egg, vinegar, and water. Pour into the dry ingredients and mix into a ball using your hands.

3. Divide the ball in half and put one half in the refrigerator. Roll out the second half on a lightly floured surface until about ⅛ inch thick and use to line the pie dish, letting the edges overhang.

4. Mix the rhubarb, sugar, flour, cinnamon, and vanilla in a large bowl and then pour it into your dough-lined dish. Dot the filled pie with the butter.

5. Thinly roll out the other piece of dough until just bigger than the top of the dish. Lay over the filling, trim off the excess dough, and pinch the top and bottom dough edges together to seal the pie. Make a few cuts in the top so the pie can breathe. Use any leftover scraps to make shapes to decorate your crust.

6. Cook in the middle of the oven for about 1 hour, checking after 40 minutes to make sure the crust doesn't burn. Cool slightly before serving.

How do plants communicate with you?

I grow rhubarb from seed on my balcony in Copenhagen. In late April, fists of leaves emerge from the soil, unfurling to serve as sun-soaking umbrellas, powering the stalks to grow. I realize it is the plant, not me, in charge of the growing process. I am the nurturer, doing my best to read its signals, like a new parent with a crying baby. I think of the human-plant relationship similarly. I provide good soil, water, shade, proximity to pollinators, and, if I read the plant's signals correctly, I am rewarded with rhubarb.

Rhubarb and Mint Sodas

We all need to give ourselves a few moments of space. I pause to connect to my inner nature as nature when I slowly sip on a homemade soda and ponder how I am in constant process of exchange. This syrup is enough for four refreshing rhubarb and mint sodas or, spiked with ¼ cup of vodka or gin, four cocktails.

Makes

1 cup syrup

Ingredients

For the syrup

1 cup sugar

1¼ cups water

1 stalk of rhubarb (about 10 ounces), chopped

For the soda

Sprig of mint

¼ cup syrup

Ice

Sparkling water

Method

1. Put the sugar and water into a saucepan over low heat and stir constantly until the sugar dissolves. Add the rhubarb and steep for 20 minutes. Strain the rhubarb and store the syrup in the refrigerator for a week. Munch the rhubarb as it is, or serve over ice cream.

2. Rub a mint leaf in your fingers to release the oil and then run it around the rim of a tall glass filled with ice. Pour in the syrup, top with sparkling water, and add the mint.

What stops you from taking time to plug in to your environment?

Sometimes all we need to connect is quiet. Carve out 20 minutes for yourself one spring day and make this drink. Marvel at the transformation of fibrous rhubarb to bittersweet syrup. Smell the mint leaves and take a deep breath. When your soda is ready, find a place outdoors or by an open window and one sip at a time make a sensual memory of the moment. Listen to the sounds around you, consider the wind, the light, the sun, and just let yourself be a human who is simply being.

Elderflower Syrup

The delicate clusters of white blossoms that emerge on elderberry (*Sambucus*) trees in late spring, emit an intoxicating aroma in the morning, which is when their favored pollinators are most active. That is the time of day to gather elderflowers. Make sure you make your syrup (sometimes labeled as a cordial on imported syrup) immediately after gathering the flowers to capture the aroma.

Makes
About 2 (750-millilter/
25.4-ounce) bottles

Ingredients
About 20 elderflower heads
Zest and juice of 1 lemon
1¾ cups sugar for every
2½ cups of steeped liquid
Sparkling wine or water,
to serve

Method

1. Dust off any insects from the elderflowers. Don't rinse the heads, however, or you will lose the fragrance. Sterilize the bottles, their stoppers, and a funnel (see page 60 for the sterilizing method.)

2. Put the elderflowers into a large saucepan and cover with enough water to completely submerge the flowers. Add the lemon zest and juice and simmer for 30 minutes, making sure the flowers remain submerged. Remove from the heat and let steep overnight.

3. The next day, strain the liquid into a saucepan through a sieve lined with cheesecloth, squeezing the flowers to extract all the liquid. Measure the liquid and for every 2½ cups, add 1¾ cups of sugar. Place the pan over low heat, stirring until the sugar has dissolved. Simmer for 3–5 minutes, skimming off any scum that rises to the surface. Pour the syrup into your bottles, using a funnel, and seal with a swing-top stopper or screw-top cap.

4. To serve, fill a chilled champagne flute one-third full with elderflower syrup and top with sparkling wine or water.

How do trees provide for your life and make your life worth living?

There was a time when we worshipped trees. How sensible! They perfume the air, purify the atmosphere, anchor and enrich soil, fill our pantry with fruit, nuts, and syrup, and provide wood to build those pantries. Give a toast of gratitude to trees with a glass of elderflower "champagne."

Eating

for

Celebration

Cultivating Humility

> "If you wish to make an apple pie from scratch, you must first invent the universe."
>
> Carl Sagan

Apple pie graces many celebratory tables at harvest time. The verb "to celebrate" comes from the Latin for "to honor." American astronomer Carl Sagan eloquently reminded us that each morsel of food we consume is the product of all the life that ever was and enables us to perpetuate the cycle. Feasting is an opportunity to honor our interdependence with all forms of life, as we devour it.

A harvest feast offers gratitude for abundance but, let's expand that story. Let's honor that from which the abundance is born; rest, struggle, collaboration, competition, determination, and acceptance of what cannot be controlled. One in one million seedlings will eventually become a completely formed tree. Most will be ground into the soil, food for microorganisms. Is one destiny more valuable than the other? There would be no fruit, no tree, no orchard if it weren't for the soil. At a mindful harvest feast, apple pie is humble pie in disguise. You, your apple pie, and the tree from which the apples grew are different recipes made from the same cosmic soup. You all require water, energy, and carbon to thrive. You are all a part of a universe that is constantly expanding. There is nothing you can do to stop change. It is inevitable. You can, however, behave in ways that restore a balance of give and take to our world. When we have all understood better how to read the language of

nature and honor ourselves through actions that respect our interdependence, we will better our chances of extending life for our own species beyond the Anthropocene. Now that is something to celebrate.

Our final chapter on eating for celebration begins at the point of the year during which the cycle of most edible life ends, because that is where the cycle begins once again. I offer to you a harvest feast of thanksgiving designed to cultivate your humility through gratitude and some questions to consider how to pay it forward.

Ritual

Ritual with Food for Celebration: Peppering Pleasure with Purpose

You could eat a slice of cake 364 days a year, because you have a sweet tooth. But when you eat that piece of cake on your birthday, it has been transformed. Your birthday cake magically embodies your life story and your future dreams, and it connects you to those you hold most dear. The act of eating has meaning way beyond providing us with fuel. Pause and consider how you celebrate with food.

- At which celebrations does eating play a big part?
- Do you choose different foods for different celebrations? Why?
- Do different celebratory foods connect you to different people and places?
- Did you make decisions about the foods you traditionally eat at celebrations, or did you inherit the menu selection as a part of your culture?
- Do you know how those foods are produced?
- Considering how those foods are produced, which elements of nature could you honor in your next celebration? How?

**Ritual with Nature
for Celebration:
Gratitude is an Attitude**

One ritual I have picked up living in Denmark is saying "Tak for Mad" when food is served. It means "Thanks for Food." It is a simple and repeated utterance that offers gratitude for the food, for the person who prepared it, and I like to think that magical collaboration of people, plants, animals, wind, water, soil, sun, and the tiniest of microscopic organisms that made every morsel possible.

If you make a habit of one ritual in this book, let it be this one. Set your intent, and with love in your heart and food in your belly, utter a simple "tak for mad" every time you eat. It is a way to honor your understanding that nature isn't out there, it's in you.

Thanksgiving Can Travel Anywhere
I learned the story of the first American Thanksgiving, which took place in 1621, as a child in Fairport, New York. When religious pilgrims from England arrived in what they called Plymouth, Massachusetts, in fall 1620, they were unprepared for winter, and almost half of those who made the journey on the *Mayflower* died. Some native Wampanoag people shared skills with the colonists to teach them to thrive. At the next harvest, the colonists held a feast of Thanksgiving to show their gratitude. Tragically, as history tells, the compassion of the native people was not reciprocated much beyond that feast. Yet, what persists in the hearts and minds of Americans is the tale of interdependence and generosity.

Thanksgiving's power to connect is so great that it first became an official national holiday when President Abraham Lincoln sought to heal a divided nation in a time of civil war. I haven't lived in the United States for nearly twenty years, but everywhere I go, I take Thanksgiving with me and find myself celebrating with people from all over the world drawn to the allure of the act of thanksgiving. Yet, if the patriotic story is meaningless, why do they celebrate Thanksgiving?

Thanksgiving speaks to our souls. It gives us a time to collectively honor ourselves (we reflect on what it is that makes us thrive and we are asked to share those thoughts), we honor others (those who have fed us, helped us, inspired us, supported us, challenged us, loved us), and we honor place (the biosphere that has nurtured the food upon which we feast and we are asked how we will pay it forward). Through the process of preparing, making, and sharing a feast, we develop a greater awareness how life itself enables us to thrive, if we choose to let it.

The recipes that follow offer a feast of Thanksgiving. Make it all at once or serve individual dishes with a "tak for mad" to bring a touch of thanksgiving to a midweek harvest meal.

Mushroom, Zucchini, and Pumpkin Seed Canapés

Ever noticed the wonder on people's faces as they hover over a tray of canapés? I think part of the awe is the shift in perspective; we don't often eat quality food on our feet. When I serve these mushroom canapés, I imagine my guests as hunter-gatherers, grazing off the forest floor.

Serves
4

Ingredients

8 medium cremini mushrooms, brushed clean

2 tablespoons olive oil

1 large onion, diced

1 zucchini, diced

3 garlic cloves, minced

2 teaspoons whole-grain mustard

Handful of pumpkin seeds (page 160), ground

⅔ cup dried bread crumbs

Pinch each of dried thyme and sage

Pinch of paprika

1 teaspoon coconut oil (optional)

Handful of fresh thyme leaves

Salt and pepper

Method

1. Preheat the oven to 375°F, unless you intend to make these in advance. Remove the mushroom stems, dice, and set aside. Put a pinch of salt and pepper inside the mushroom caps, rub the outside with olive oil, and place, cap side down, on a baking sheet.

2. Warm the rest of the oil in a skillet and sauté the onion for 3 minutes before adding the zucchini and mushroom stems. Cook for another 3 minutes, then add the garlic and mustard. Cook for 1 minute. Remove from the heat and add the pumpkin seeds, bread crumbs, herbs, and paprika. Taste. I often add a teaspoon of coconut oil or olive oil at this stage. If time allows, let the stuffing sit for several hours to enhance the flavor.

3. Stuff each mushroom and bake for 15–20 minutes, until the caps brown and soften. Remove from the oven and sprinkle with fresh thyme before serving.

Tip The amount of stuffing here is probably more than you need; any leftovers can be cooked and served separately.

How do our eating choices contribute to the life cycle?

Mushrooms are the fruits of mycelium, organisms that provide a tissuelike structure for forests to improve water and nutrient absorption and disease resistance for plants and trees. Mycelial colonies can extend for acres and are among the largest living organisms on the earth. By cutting off the nutrient and water supply to flora, fauna, and soil, mycelium can deplete entire forests with the purpose of instigating renewal.

Vegan Creamed Corn

No harvest feast is complete without corn of some variety. Fitting, because there would be no corn as we know it today without human intervention in the form of agriculture. Nature develops in response to other forms of nature. It is a constant dance.

Serves
4 as a side

Ingredients
1 tablespoon coconut oil

3 cups corn kernels, fresh or frozen

1 tablespoon sugar

1 tablespoon cornstarch

¼ cup water, at room temperature

½ cup coconut milk

Pepper

Method
1. Heat the coconut oil in a saucepan over medium heat. Add the corn kernels and sauté for 2–3 minutes or until it is warmed through and softened—try a kernel to test. Stir in the sugar and pepper. Cook until the liquid is absorbed by the corn.

2. Blend the cornstarch with the water in a small bowl as if you were making gravy—no lumps! Gradually add to the corn, stirring continuously. Add the coconut milk, reduce the heat, and cook until thickened. Season and serve.

How is your curiosity fired by your relationship with nature?
More than 9,000 years ago, people in Central America looked at wild grass and discovered that the evolutionary magic of cross pollination could produce what today we call corn, or sweet corn. Over the millennia, nomads and traders spread kernels of sweet corn around the globe, a journey documented in corn's genomic scrapbook; corn possesses 12,000 more genes than a human being. Imagine the people, plants, pests, and paradises corn met along the way to being planted in cornfields so vast they can be seen from space.

Garlic Truffled Mashed Potatoes

Here, I team the unctuous mashed potatoes with the oil from a pungent fungus still much considered a luxury in our times—the truffle. Delicious, rare, and highly valued, truffles have a story to share that reminds us to honor the interdependence of all of nature.

Serves
6

Ingredients

1 head of garlic

2 tablespoons olive oil

4 large starchy potatoes (such as Yukon Gold or russets), cubed

½ cup vegetable broth (page 108)

¼ cup oat milk

2 tablespoons butter or coconut oil

¼ cup truffle oil, plus extra to serve

Salt and pepper

Method

1. Preheat the oven to 400°F and line a baking sheet with parchment paper.

2. To roast the garlic, cut the tip off the head to expose the cloves, put it onto the lined sheet, and drizzle with the oil. Use the paper to wrap the garlic into a bundle and roast for 25 minutes.

3. Put the potatoes into a saucepan, cover with water, and bring to a boil, then simmer for 20 minutes, until soft. Drain well and return to the pan.

4. Squeeze the roasted garlic cloves out of their skins into a bowl and mash. Add the broth, milk, butter or coconut oil, and truffle oil and mix together. Gradually pour the liquid over the potatoes and mash until the potatoes are creamy and fluffy. (I keep them unpeeled; this adds texture to the dish.) Season to taste. Add a drizzle of truffle oil before serving.

What do luxurious truffles teach us about humility?

Truffles grow underground and need help from mobile animals to reproduce. So truffles learned to replicate the aroma of boar pheromones, which no able-snouted gilt in heat can resist! After the animal eats the truffles, the spores are spread in its dung, helping the fungus to multiply. We must be careful if we want our love affair with truffles to continue, because weather conditions related to climate change have caused a marked decline in European truffle harvests in the past one hundred years.

Oven-roasted Brussels Sprouts

Brussels sprouts enjoy pride of place on feasting tables way beyond Belgium, and rightly so. This robust brassica is harvested late because sprouts remain on their stems after reaching maturity, which is preferable—they will taste sweeter.

Serves
4 as a side

Ingredients

1 pound Brussels sprouts, trimmed

3 tablespoons extra virgin olive oil

½ teaspoon crushed red pepper flakes

Salt and pepper

Pickled pumpkin (page 164) or preserved lemon (page 38), chopped, to serve

Method

1. Preheat the oven to 400°F.

2. Check the Brussels sprouts and peel off any outer leaves with dirt or insects and add to your compost bin. Mix the oil and red pepper flakes with a pinch of salt and pepper in a small dish. Spread the sprouts evenly on a baking sheet and drizzle with the oil mix. Toss them with a spoon a few times to evenly distribute the oil. Roast for 30–40 minutes, turning a few times. The outer leaves will become crispy, but the inner sprout should stay tender.

3. Season and mix with pickled pumpkin or the rind of a preserved lemon before serving.

> **Which is hardier, humans or Brussels sprouts?**
> How often do you look at a vegetable and feel inspired by its resilience? When you think about how plants withstand heat, storms, and frost, it is hard not to marvel at their strength. When it comes to immune-boosting winter foods, such as Brussels sprouts, there is no denying that, physically, we derive much of our resilience from theirs. Maybe our mental resilience, too.

Maple-roasted Carrots

More often than not, there is a small pitcher of maple syrup in my kitchen. It is used sparingly and treated as an absolute luxury that I import from the northeastern American land where I was born. When I do use it, I like to ponder the mystery of how humans came to discover tree sap.

Serves
4 as a side

Ingredients
6 carrots (about 1 pound)
1 tablespoon granola oil
2 tablespoons maple syrup
Salt

Method

1. Preheat the oven to 400°F. Put a baking sheet in the oven to warm. Peel and chop the carrots into chunks, on the diagonal. Reserve the peels for your broth box (page 108) or to make carrot powder (see recipe facing page).

2. Toss the carrots with the oil and a pinch of salt, spread on the baking sheet, and roast for 15 minutes. Remove, pour the maple syrup over them, and roast for another 20 minutes. Remove when the carrots have browned and are soft. Season to serve.

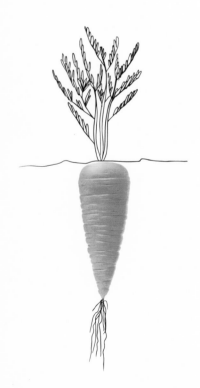

What value does syrup provide for the maple tree?

Legend tells that maple syrup was discovered when a Native American threw a hatchet at a tree and out poured sugary gold. But don't picture a geyser exploding! Sap flows are prompted by the change in atmospheric conditions when the winter thaw begins. This triggers sap to flow to bring nutrients up from the roots and circulate stored sugar, which provides the energy for spring to be sprung. It is more probable that rapt attention to the small details of the cycle of life led to the discovery of maple syrup.

Zero-waste Carrot Powder

In the spirit of honoring our interdependence on things we usually think of as mundane, don't toss your carrot peels. Instead, dry them, grind them, and transform them into a powder. I find that the peels pack an intensely earthy and carroty flavor. I use the powder to dust soups, salads, add to bread dough, and rim whiskey glasses, as one would a margarita.

Ingredients

Carrot peels

Method

1. Each time you have carrot peels, store them in a freezer container. When full, thaw and dehydrate. If you have a dehydrator, spread out the peel and use the vegetable setting. Otherwise, place the peels on a wire cooling rack, allowing some space between them so that air reaches all sides. Turn the oven to its lowest setting, place your rack on a baking sheet, and let the peels dry for 5–6 hours. They are ready when dry to the touch but not yet brittle.

2. Process in a food processor or coffee grinder to a powder. Store in an airtight jar for up to three months.

> ### How do you honor your relationship with food when you eat?
> *"Les carottes sont cuites. Je répète. Les carottes sont cuites."* ("The carrots are cooked. I repeat. The carrots are cooked.") So began the BBC broadcast on June 5, 1944, enigmatically alerting the French that the Invasion of Normandy had begun. Never rationed, carrots were praised for supposedly enhancing the eyesight needed during blackouts and raids. Resourceful cooks turned carrots into cakes, Indian curries, and Christmas puddings. Carrots represented honor. To honor carrots, I waste not by making this zero-waste carrot powder.

Butter

Making butter is a simple process we don't need to delegate to industry. Going through the motions with intent helps to kindle new respect for ourselves as nature, and for domesticated animals, such as cows, which have been part of the human story for millennia.

Makes
About ½ cup (4 ounces—the same as 1 stick)

Ingredients
1 cup heavy cream

> ### How can you honor your natural heritage as you cook?
>
> Energy can be transformed but not destroyed, as knew every milkmaid ever. Lending elbow grease to a churn heats cream, and as molecules move faster, the dense fat molecules clump together, separate from buttermilk, and a butterball is born.

Method

1. Select a clean, screw-top jar that can hold double the amount of liquid, but not much more. Remove the cream from the refrigerator an hour beforehand; it needs to be warm. Pour the cream into the jar, filling it halfway. Screw the lid on tightly. Shake vigorously for 7–10 minutes. After about 4 minutes, you should have whipped cream. After 6 minutes, you should start to hear a ball sloshing in liquid. Shake for another minute.

2. Set a fine-mesh sieve over a bowl and pour the contents out of the jar. Place the butterball in a bowl and bathe it with a few teaspoons of water as you knead it gently to squeeze out all the buttermilk, so that the butter will last longer. Mold your butter into shape, and put it into the refrigerator until ready to serve. You can drink your buttermilk, or use it in baking or the stuffing recipe (facing page).

Maple Butter

Forests, soil, grasses, farms, and human and natural history all combine to make this decadent celebration spread.

Serves
8 as a spread

Ingredients
¼ cup maple syrup
½ cup (4 ounces) butter (see above)
Pinch of salt

Method

1. Put the maple syrup into a small saucepan with a pinch of salt and bring to a boil. Remove from the heat, stir in the butter until it melts, then whisk for 10 minutes, until the texture is fluffy. Refrigerate to harden. As it cools, the butter may separate. If it has, stir before serving.

Buttermilk Herbed Stuffing

When you separate the fat solids from the rest of your cream, you end up with tangy buttermilk. Combine it with day-old bread for a new take on a traditional side dish that's destined to steal the show.

Serves

5 as a side

Ingredients

2 tablespoons unsalted butter (see recipe facing page)

1 red onion, chopped

2 celery sticks, thinly sliced

1 tablespoon chopped rosemary leaves

1 tablespoon chopped sage leaves

1 tablespoon thyme leaves

½ teaspoon freshly ground black pepper

12 ounces chanterelle or other seasonal mushrooms, chopped

½ cup vegetable broth (page 108)

7 slices sourdough bread (day-old is perfect), rubbed into crumbs

½ cup buttermilk (from the butter recipe, facing page)

1 egg

Method

1. Melt the butter in a large skillet and add the onions. Once they have softened, about 6 minutes, add the celery, herbs, and pepper. Cook for another 4 minutes, then add the mushrooms. It will take about 5 minutes for the mushrooms to become tender, depending on how crowded they are. Once tender, add the broth and simmer for 10 minutes. Add the bread, buttermilk, and egg and mix until the bread is coated.

2. Let cool, then refrigerate the stuffing for a day to let the flavors develop. Preheat oven to 400°F and grease a medium baking dish. Transfer the stuffing to the dish and bake 20–30 minutes, until golden brown on top.

> **How does our behavior in one season ensure our survival in the next?**
>
> When we stuff ourselves at winter feasts, culture mirrors nature: we're fattening ourselves for the lean season. If rations are thin in spring, we'll be hungry but we'll have energy to burn. To honor our seasonal selves, add stuffing to vegetarian feasts. While the Roman chef Apicius in the pages of *De re Coquinaria* ("On the Subject of Cooking") stuffed everything, even a dormouse, archaeological evidence indicates that stuffing was also prepared as a vegetarian side dish.

Short and Stout Bread

Bread baking is transformative—a process you nurture, with the help of yeast and heat. You can leave all the heavy lifting to yeast if you bake bread with beer!

Makes
1 9 x 5-inch loaf

Ingredients

2 tablespoons canola oil, plus extra for greasing

1¾ cups whole-wheat flour

1¾ cups all-purpose flour

2 tablespoons whole-grain mustard

1½ teaspoons salt

1 teaspoon baking soda

1 teaspoon baking powder

Pinch each of chili powder, paprika, cumin, thyme, and oregano

1 extra-large egg

1½ cups stout

Method

1. Preheat the oven to 350°F and lightly grease and line the bottom of a 9 x 5-inch loaf pan.

2. Mix together the flours, mustard, salt, baking soda, baking powder, and spices in a large bowl. In a smaller bowl, mix the oil, egg, and beer. Add the wet ingredients to the dry ingredients and stir to combine.

3. Transfer the dough to the loaf pan and bake for 45 minutes. Remove from the oven and let cool in the pan on a wire rack before turning the loaf out of the pan.

How can we feast to create bonds with the natural world?

Feasting, lubricated by beer, is a centuries-old ritual that has been used by humans to create bonds. As feasting became a cornerstone of culture, we cemented our bonds with one another and a bevy of other life-forms, including yeast, the single-celled fungi afloat in the air that gives rise to our bread and makes our beer foam. Baking beer bread heightens my awareness of all the invisible life that shape my own experience. Climate change and environmental degradation impact on microorganisms as much as on those we can see. How will that change our lives?

Spiced Pumpkin and Coconut Soup

Serves
6

Ingredients
1 large Halloween pumpkin
1 small Hokkaido pumpkin
1 tablespoon canola oil
1 onion, chopped
1 head of garlic, cloves separated and chopped
½ chile, chopped
2 bay leaves
1 tablespoon ground cumin
½ tablespoon ground cinnamon
1 tablespoon ground ginger
1 cup white wine
2 cups vegetable broth (page 108)
1¾ cups coconut milk

While serving pumpkin soup in its hollowed-out skin is not essential, it is a visual cue to diners to pay homage to the cycle of life and all the elements of nature that enable you and the pumpkin to thrive.

Method
1. Cut a circle in the top of your Halloween pumpkin and scoop out the seeds and fibers. Save all the seeds for roasting (recipe below). Remove as much flesh as possible but leave enough so that the skin can serve as a stable tureen. Peel and chop your Hokkaido pumpkin. In total, you need about 9 cups of prepared flesh.

2. Warm the oil in a large stockpot and cook the onion, garlic, and chile until soft, about 3 minutes. Add the pumpkin flesh, bay leaves, spices, wine, and broth. Bring to a boil and simmer for 30 minutes. Add the coconut milk and simmer for another 10 minutes. Remove the bay leaves and using a handheld mixer, blend to a creamy consistency.

3. Serve the soup in the pumpkin tureen, sprinkled with roasted pumpkin seeds. After serving the soup, rinse out the pumpkin tureen. The following day, cut up the flesh, roast it with a tablespoon of olive oil, and serve it with a drizzle of tahini (page 25) and a sprinkling of parsley.

How to Roast Pumpkin Seeds
1. Preheat the oven to 350°F. Rinse the seeds to remove all the fibers and pat them dry. Transfer to a bowl and coat with 2 tablespoons of olive oil. Add ½ teaspoon of ground cumin and a pinch of salt.

2. Spread out on a baking sheet and roast for 10–15 minutes or until they are golden brown, keeping a close eye. Let cool, then transfer to an airtight container.

Why are you grateful for food?

What's the worth of thick-skinned pumpkins? When harvested and placed in a cool dry place, they stay resiliently nourishing throughout the winter. And is it sheer coincidence that these late-season bloomers are also packed with immune system boosting beta-carotene? From the pumpkin's resilience, comes your resilience.

Pumpkin Pie Bars

Makes
12–18 bars

Ingredients
For the crust

5 tablespoons melted butter or coconut oil, plus extra for greasing

1 cup rolled oats

1⅓ cups whole-wheat flour

1 teaspoon ground cinnamon

¼ teaspoon salt

2 tablespoons apple molasses (page 171) or honey

3 tablespoons maple syrup

2 eggs

For the filling

½ cup packed brown sugar

1 teaspoon ground cinnamon

1 teaspoon ground ginger

½ teaspoon freshly grated nutmeg

½ teaspoon ground cloves

½ teaspoon mace

½ teaspoon salt

3 eggs

1 cup oat milk or peanut milk (page 86)

1 (15½-ounce) can of pumpkin or 1 Hokkaido pumpkin or butternut squash (about 1½ pounds), peeled, seeded, and cut into chunks

As the song goes: "There's a happy feeling nothing in the world can buy, when they pass around the coffee and the pumpkin pie." For centuries, we have honored the harvest with this stick-to-your-ribs treat.

Method

1. To stew your own pumpkin, put the prepared flesh into a saucepan with ½ cup of water, bring to a boil, then cover the pan and simmer for 20–30 minutes, until the pumpkin is tender. Drain and mash the pumpkin. Set aside to cool.

2. Preheat the oven to 400°F and grease a 12 x 9-inch baking pan. To make the crust, put the oats into a food processor and grind to a coarse flour, then add it to a mixing bowl with the whole-wheat flour, cinnamon, and salt. In a separate bowl, whisk the melted butter or oil with the apple molasses or honey, maple syrup and eggs. Fold the wet into the dry ingredients.

3. Transfer the dough to the pan and press into an even layer, making sure you fill the corners. Lay a piece of parchment paper on top, fill with pie weights or dried beans, and bake for 10 minutes.

4. Meanwhile, make the filling by combining the sugar, spices, and salt in a bowl. Whisk the eggs in a separate bowl, stir in the milk, then fold into the sugar and spices. Add the pumpkin and mix until smooth.

5. Remove the pan from the oven, take out the weights and paper, and pour the filling over the crust. Return to the oven, reduce the temperature to 350°F, and cook for about 30 minutes. The pie is done when the filling starts to brown and feels spongy but firm to the touch. Cut into bars while still warm.

Why do humans use feasts to perpetuate culture?

For decades, Sarah Josepha Hale, an abolitionist, author, and editor in nineteenth-century North America, campaigned to have Thanksgiving declared a unifying national holiday. In her novel *Northwood*, she wrote that at Thanksgiving, "the pumpkin pie occupied the most distinguished niche." Perhaps because the dish so deeply ties people to time and to place.

Pickled Pumpkin

Makes
1 (1-quart) jar

Ingredients
1 cup plus 2 tablespoons sugar
1 cup white wine vinegar
2 cinnamon sticks
8 whole cloves
3 tablespoons mustard seeds
6½ cups peeled and diced
pumpkin

Pickling pumpkin with intent is a great way to consider what it is that you aim to preserve as you embark on the making process. Sure, as an outcome you'll have pumpkin for salads, snacks, and sandwiches throughout the winter. But the making process is even more important for honoring time, place, heritage, and your part in the cycle of life. What are you trying to preserve? What are you trying to innovate?

Method
1. Put the sugar, vinegar, cinnamon, cloves, and mustard seeds into a large saucepan. Bring to a boil, add the pumpkin, and simmer for 20 minutes.

2. Meanwhile, process your canning jars according to the directions on page 60.

3. Spoon the pumpkin into each jar and fill with the pickling liquid, making sure that you leave a ½-inch gap at the top. Immediately place sterilized lids on each filled jar and seal. When all the jars are sealed, process them to keep them shelf-stable for up to six months (follow the directions on page 60).

How do you honor yourself when you honor other forms of life?

"It would be becoming of us to speak modestly of our place in the universe. Let me offer a metaphor. Earth relates to the universe as the second segment of the left antenna of an aphid sitting on a flower petal in the garden in Teaneck, New Jersey, for a few hours this afternoon." E. O. Wilson

Native American agrarians cultivated personal humility as they nurtured regenerative food systems. The "Three Sisters" (corn, beans, and pumpkins) represented a microcosm of the food web they served. Corn was planted to provide a trellis upon which soil-feeding (nitrogen-fixing) beans would weave their way to the sky, while helping to support the corn stalks during storms. Pumpkins would grow in the shade of the corn and, as they plumped, would help to retain moisture in the soil during scorching summers. It's a tale I consider when I pickle pumpkin for seasonal gifts to reinforce my intent to develop a nature-relatedness practice to become the change from head to hands to habit.

Tart and Tangy Wild Berry Sauce

Cranberries were apparently shared by Native Americans and settlers at the first Thanksgiving meal in 1621, thanks to the Native Americans' foraging abilities. Astute observers and experimenters in their North American environment, Native Americans ate wild cranberries long before the fruit's association with the feasting day.

Serves
6

Ingredients
3⅔ cups cranberries
⅔ cup sugar
⅔ cup red wine
1 cinnamon stick
2 star anise
1 tablespoon orange zest
1 teaspoon freshly grated ginger

Method
1. Wash and pick over the berries. Combine the sugar, wine, cinnamon, anise, orange zest, and ginger in a saucepan. Bring to a boil until the sugar is dissolved and the wine slightly reduced. Add the berries and simmer until the sauce has thickened, which takes 10–15 minutes.

2. Remove from the heat. Fish out the cinnamon sticks and star anise. Mash the sauce if necessary. Refrigerate before serving.

3. If you want to increase the quantities to make more sauce for another day, process by following the directions on page 60.

> **Why do you think some wild plants were more easily domesticated than others?**
> If you have access to organic cranberries to serve at your Thanksgiving feast, go for it! If not, take the road less traveled to make a difference. Wild cranberries don't take well to domestication and dangerous toxins that poison water systems are poured into bogs to enable a controlled harvest. If you love how the tart cranberry cuts the richness of a feast, opt for any tangy organic or foraged berry instead. Sea buckthorn, chokeberries, lingonberries, blackberries, and even blueberries will do.

Baked Sweet Potato and Apple

Baked sweet potato and apple was a holiday tradition in my childhood home, concocted by my dad. It brings together savory and sweet with warming winter spices, the smell of which take me immediately back to upstate New York in the 1980s—wherever I am.

Serves
4 as a side

Ingredients
1 tablespoon coconut oil, plus extra for greasing

2 small to medium sweet potatoes, peeled and cut into slices about ½ inch thick

2 apples, cored and sliced thinly

Juice of 2 oranges (you need about ½ cup)

2 tablespoons ginger juice

2 teaspoons ground cinnamon

2 tablespoons rosemary leaves

Sugar

Pinch of salt

Method

1. Preheat the oven to 350°F and grease a medium baking dish. Bring a saucepan of water to a boil and add the sweet potato slices. Bring back to a boil, cook for 3 minutes, drain, then cool.

2. Form a layer of sweet potatoes and apples in the pan as if making a lasagne. Mix the coconut oil with the juices and the cinnamon. Sprinkle the juices, rosemary, and a dash of sugar on each layer. Continue to form layers until all the ingredients are used, reserving some liquid to drizzle over the top layer. Cover the dish and bake for 30–40 minutes, until soft and starting to brown.

3. Serve warm with other savory dishes in this chapter.

How does eating connect us to place?

Sweet potato is neither a potato nor a yam. It is a member of the morning glory family Convolvulaceae, with a lineage that is thought to go back 57 million years. Africans introduced yams to the Americas when slave traders forced their relocation. Their yams didn't prosper, so they nurtured the native sweet potatoes, which are similar tasting. Sweet potato, which has few pests or diseases and grows well in sandier soil, became a reliable staple that connected people to places near and far. It is honored with extra sweet treatment when it graces a Thanksgiving table.

Spiced Applesauce

From the "forbidden fruit" to Newton's apple, for different people in different cultures, apples represent temptation, intelligence, eternal life, death, sin, and even national identity. Part of food culture is using food as a reference for the human condition. Why that is the case is something to stew on as this applesauce cooks.

Serves
10

Ingredients
8 tart apples (such as McIntosh, Pippin, or Braeburn)
¼ cup water
2 tablespoons honey
1 teaspoon ground cinnamon
1 teaspoon ground ginger
½ teaspoon freshly grated nutmeg
½ teaspoon ground cloves

Method

1. Peel and core the apples, reserving the peel to make apple powder (follow the directions on page 155). Chop the apples into chunks.

2. Bring the water and honey to a boil in a saucepan, then reduce the heat to a simmer. Add the apples and spices and simmer for 20–30 minutes, until the apples become mushy and the water content reduces. Use a fork to mash. Serve warm or chilled. Keep some in a container in the freezer for up to two months.

> **What cultural associations or phrases come to your mind when you consider apples?**
> Bio-artist Joe Davis has been working with geneticists to encode all of Wikipedia into the genomes of apples to create an orchard that documents humanity. Literally and figuratively, we humans derive a lot of meaning from apples, and it goes way beyond the food on our plate.

Apple Molasses

There are more than 7,500 known apple varieties on the earth. The variance of tastes and textures are arguably as complex as fine wines. Unsurprisingly, then, you can use apples for purposes you have yet to consider, including molasses made from local cider.

Makes

4 (10-ounce) jars

Ingredients

4–8 quarts unfiltered nonalcoholic apple juice or cider, or use a low-alcohol cider from a local producer

1 cinnamon stick

Method

1. Pour the juice or cider into a heavy, nonreactive saucepan that is large enough for the liquid to boil vigorously. Add the cinnamon stick. Slowly bring to a boil, reduce the heat, and simmer for 3 hours, stirring and skimming occasionally. The end of the reduction requires constant stirring to prevent scorching. Your molasses is done when it coats the back of a spoon and has the consistency of maple syrup. It will be about one-tenth of its original volume—his is necessary for your molasses to be shelf stable.

2. Boil bottles or jars to sterilize them (page 60) before adding your molasses. Once opened, keep the molasses in the refrigerator for up to six months.

> ### How can you celebrate biodiversity when you cook?
>
> As observers at the World Wildlife Fund have explained: "Sugar has had as great an impact on the environment as any other agricultural commodity. Wholesale conversion of habitat on tropical islands and in coastal areas has led to significant environmental damage—particularly a loss of biodiversity." Making apple molasses using unfiltered apple juice or cider from a local mill provides an alternative. Baking with intent honors the cacophony of biodiverse life that makes yours sweeter.

Apple Molasses and Goat Cheese Pancakes

Maple syrup isn't produced in most parts of the world, but apples are. Add some sweetness to a winter's night by making these savory pancakes topped with apple molasses made from a locally produced cider.

Makes
8 pancakes

Ingredients
1⅔ cups all-purpose flour

1 teaspoon baking powder

Leaves from a few fresh thyme sprigs, chopped, or 1 teaspoon dried thyme

2 teaspoons zero-waste carrot powder (page 155)

1 egg

1¼ cups oat milk or buttermilk (page 156)

⅔ cup crumbled goat cheese

2 tablespoons canola oil

To serve
Apple molasses (page 171)

Spiced applesauce (page 170)

Fresh thyme sprigs

Method

1. Mix together the flour, baking powder, thyme, carrot powder, and a pinch of salt. In a separate bowl, beat the egg and mix with the milk. Combine the dry and wet ingredients to form a batter. Cool in the refrigerator for 15–20 minutes before mixing crumbled goat cheese into the batter.

2. Heat one-quarter of the oil in a large skillet and add a ladleful of pancake batter. In 2–3 minutes, bubbles will appear on the surface, indicating that it's ready to be flipped. Cook on the other side for 2–3 minutes or until golden. When the pancake is cooked, put it on a plate, covered with a dish towel to keep warm, while you make the rest. Depending on the size of your pan, you may be able to make several at a time.

3. Plate up the pancakes, drizzle with apple molasses, and serve with a dollop of applesauce and fresh thyme.

How is winter an important part of the cycle of life?
Before electricity, humans had no choice but to do less in the dark winter, and meals would have been mainly comprised of preserved foods. In winter, take some of your days as slow as molasses while you linger over these pancakes. Before you do, stand outside your door, take a few deep breaths, and try to align your inner pace with that of the nonhuman life that surrounds you.

Apple Molasses Gingerbread Cookies

The idea of gingerbread men started in sixteenth-century England, an age in which spices, such as ginger, cinnamon, and cloves, were luxuries. Legend has it that Queen Elizabeth I asked for gingerbread to be served in the shapes of visiting dignitaries to demonstrate hospitality while reminding visitors of her power and wealth.

Makes
36

Ingredients

¾ cup (6 ounces) butter (page 156)

¾ cup plus 2 tablespoons sugar (preferably beet sugar; choose what is local to you)

⅓ cup ginger syrup or light corn syrup

generous 1 cup apple molasses (page 171)

1 teaspoon salt

2 teaspoons ground cinnamon

2 teaspoons ground ginger

¼ teaspoon allspice or ground cloves

1 extra-large egg

1 teaspoon baking powder

½ teaspoon baking soda

3¼ cups all-purpose flour, plus extra for rolling

Method

1. Mix together the butter, sugar, ginger syrup, apple molasses, salt, and spices, then beat in the egg. Combine the dry ingredients in a bowl. Pour in the wet ingredients and mix to form a dough. Cut the dough in half, put into airtight containers, and place in the refrigerator to firm up for at least 2 hours.

2. Once the dough has hardened, preheat the oven to 350°F and line 2–3 baking sheets with parchment paper.

3. Flour a clean surface and roll one of your pieces of dough into a rectangle ¼ inch thick. Dip a 2¼-inch cookie cutter in flour, cut out shapes, and space apart on the baking sheets. (Or simply pull off chunks of dough, roll into a ball slightly smaller than a golf ball, and flatten with your thumb.) Repeat with the second piece of dough. Bake for 8–12 minutes, or until the cookies feel firm to the touch. Keep a close eye to check that the edges do not burn. Cool and store in an airtight container.

> **How can you honor your environment when you bake gingerbread?**
> I consider sugar as a luxury good, and I tend to bake on only rare occasions, because limiting sugar is as good for the planet in terms of minimizing ecosystem destruction as it is for people. Even locally sourced beet sugar is only better than imported cane sugar if it isn't produced as a monocrop. Usually, I opt for the sweetness of homemade apple molasses instead.

Apple Shrub

Makes
4 (10-ounce) jars

Ingredients
2 small tart apples (such as Braeburn or McIntosh)
¼ cup freshly grated ginger root
1 cup sugar
1 cup apple cider vinegar

At one time, shrubs were believed to have medicinal properties and provided a good source of acidity for cooking before people had access to lemons year-round.

Method
1. Grate the unpeeled apples and mix with the ginger, sugar, and vinegar. Let the shrub ferment for three days.

2. Strain through a sieve set over a bowl to separate the apples and ginger from the liquid and squeeze the apples dry. Pour the shrub into clean jars and keep in the refrigerator for up to a week.

Temptation Preservation Cocktail

Makes
1

Ingredients
3 tablespoons whiskey (I use single malt Glenlivet)
1 tablespoon vodka
1 tablespoon apple shrub
2 teaspoons apple molasses (page 171)
Ice

Optional
For a nonalcoholic tipple, omit the liquor and top with sparkling water

This cocktail requires two homemade preserves, apple shrub and apple molasses, so plan ahead.

Method
1. Fill a martini glass with ice to chill. Add ice to your cocktail shaker. Add the whiskey, vodka, apple shrub, and apple molasses. Now add the ice from your glass to the cocktail shaker, put the top on, and SHAKE!

2. Strain into the glass. Add a cinnamon stick for sensual panache.

> **What relation with nature will you preserve from your feast?**
> Feasts exist to raise our spirits, and spirits have always been part of feasting. A tipple or two creates feelings of freedom and that freedom helps to form bonds to people, time, and place. Here's to raising a glass to the cacophony of autumnal life and how endings are the magic makers of new beginnings.

Resources

Glossary

blanching Briefly boiling a food, whether to loosen the skin or to kill enzymes or to set the color of a food or remove strong or bitter flavors.

blending A simple, handheld immersion blender or a freestanding blender achieves a smooth consistency, whereas a food processor is suitable for chopping and combining but tends to achieve a more textured result. When time allows, there is pleasure to be derived from using a simple wooden spoon or rubbing cooked ingredients through a sieve or potato ricer.

blind-baking A technique used to precook pastry before filling to make sure it is cooked properly. Pastry shells should be chilled for at least half an hour before blind-baking and cooked in a hot oven (400°F). The shell is usually lined with parchment paper and pie weights—or dried beans or uncooked rice—to hold its shape while it bakes.

chilling Cooling food in a refrigerator but not freezing it. Chilling dough, for example, before rolling allows for the fat to solidify, making the dough easier to work. See also **refreshing**.

chopping The task of preparing ingredients is a mindful action in itself, an opportunity to consider the shape, texture, size as well as flavor that an ingredient brings to a meal. A sharp knife and a solid wooden cutting board give as a good a result as a mechanical device. Allow yourself some mindful thoughts and enjoy the rhythm of the chopping action.

dried beans A culinary term, the collective name for the edible seeds of legumes that have been shelled and dried. They are invaluable in the mindful kitchen pantry where they will last for many months and, once rehydrated, readily transform into soups, stews, falafels, dips, and salads. These beans are also ground into gluten-free flours for making flatbreads.

fermentation A chemical reaction produced by enzymes, such as natural yeasts or baking soda, that causes effervescence, which makes bread rise and gives pickles their pleasing tang. Correctly made, fermentation is a way of preserving fresh ingredients, extending their life for lean months when mindful cooks are resourceful ones.

griddle A flat metal cooking utensil used to bake flatbreads or pancakes on the stove.

grill pan A heavy, usually cast-iron, pan with a ridged bottom that provides a good, even heat suitable for grilling vegetables on the stove using only a little oil.

legumes The common term for the plants of the Fabaceae family, all of which have a seed pod. They include all the beans, peas, chickpeas, lentils, and, despite the name, peanuts, as well as crops such as clover and alfalfa. Legumes are a vital crop for the soil, because they "fix" nitrogen in the soil, making sure its fertility is maintained and that cropping the land is sustainable. Versatile and delicious to eat, fresh or dried, nutritionally they are a valuable source of protein in a plant-based diet.

In culinary terms, legumes are often referred to as dried **beans**. An important bean for the mindful kitchen is the fava bean, a large, oval pale green bean that is often sold shelled and dried. Much used in Middle Eastern cuisine, these humble beans are undemanding in their growing needs and so widely cultivated—look for locally sourced fava beans instead of imported ones.

marinade A combination of oil, wine, or vinegar and spices, herbs, and sometimes garlic used to flavor ingredients that may be left to marinate in the mixture for several hours.

mincing A method of finely chopping garlic before cooking using a knife so that, unlike crushing a clove to a wet puree using a press, the pungent flavor enhances instead of overwhelms a dish. Use the side of your knife to press the clove flat, then pass the blade over it multiple times to reduce it to finely chopped pieces. Where garlic is to be used raw, simply slice or use a clove whole for a more subtle flavor.

reducing Concentrating liquid by boiling it so that the excess liquid evaporates to make a sauce or preserve, such as jam.

refreshing Rapidly cooling hot food, such as tomatoes or asparagus, by putting it under cold running water or plunging into a bowl of iced water, then draining. This stops any further cooking and helps to set the color.

soaking An essential step in the preparation of dried beans, or other dry ingredients, such as mushrooms, in order to rehydrate them completely prior to cooking. Normally, the ingredient needs to be covered in plenty of cold water and, in the case of dried beans, the soaking period can be up to 24 hours.

vegetarian cheese Not all cheeses, particularly the hard varieties, are suitable for vegetarians, because they contain animal rennet, an enzyme used to separate the solid curds in milk from the whey. Look for vegetarian-friendly alternatives that use vegetable rennet or microbial enzymes in the cheese-making process.

Further Reading

Arsenault, Chris "Only 60 Years of Farming Left if Soil Degradation Continues," *Scientific American* (December 4, 2017) www.scientificamerican.com/article/only-60-years-of-farming-left-if-soil-degradation-continues/

Blythman, Joanna "Can Hipsters Stomach the Unpalatable Truth about Avocado Toast?," *The Guardian* (August 12, 2016) www.theguardian.com/commentisfree/2016/aug/12/hispters-handle-unpalatable-truth-avocado-toast

Begdache, Lina, Maher Chaar, Nasim Sabounchi, and Hamed Kianmehr "Assessment of Dietary Factors, Dietary Practices and Exercise on Mental Distress in Young Adults Versus Matured Adults: A Cross-sectional Study," *Nutritional Neuroscience* (2017) DOI: 10.1080/1028415X.2017.1411875

Carroll, Sean B. "Tracking the Ancestry of Corn Back 9,000 Years," *The New York Times* (May 24, 2010) www.nytimes.com/2010/05/25/science/25creature.html

FAO *Women: Users, Preservers and Managers of Agrobiodiversity* (United Nations, Food and Agriculture Organization, 1999) www.fao.org/FOCUS/E/Women/Biodiv-e.htm

FAO *Status of the World´s Soil Resources (SWSR)*, Intergovernmental Technical Panel on Soils (United Nations Food and Agriculture Organization, 2015) www.fao.org/documents/card/en/c/c6814873-efc3-41db-b7d3-2081a10ede50/

FAO *Year of Soil*, Factsheet (United Nations, Food and Agriculture Organization, 2015) www.fao.org/soils-2015/news/news-detail/en/c/277682/ sourced on 03012019

FAO *Second Report on the State of the World´s Plant Genetic Resources* (United Nations, Food and Agriculture Organization, 2018) www.fao.org/agriculture/crops/thematic-sitemap/theme/seeds-pgr/sow/sow2/press-releases/en/

Frischmann, Chad "The Climate Impact of the Food in the Back of Your Fridge," *The Washington Post* (July 31, 2018) www.washingtonpost.com/news/theworldpost/wp/2018/07/31/food-waste/?utm_term=.08baf2503397

Grooten, M. and R. E. A. Almond *Living Planet Report – 2018: Aiming Higher* (World Wildlife Fund, 2018)

Hamblin, James "The Dark Side of Almond Use," *The Atlantic* (August 28, 2014) www.theatlantic.com/health/archive/2014/08/almonds-demon-nuts/379244/

Herz, Rachel *Why You Eat What You Eat: The Science Behind Our Relationship with Food* (W. W. Norton & Co., 2018)

Holden, Patrick "Is Eating No Meat Actually Doing More Harm Than Good?," *Sustainable Food Trust* (11 May 2017) sustainablefoodtrust.org/articles/is-eating-no-meat-actually-doing-more-harm-than-good/

IPCC *Special Report on Global Warming of 1.5°C* (Intergovernmental Panel on Climate Change, 2018) www.ipcc.ch/2018/10/08/summary-for-policymakers-of-ipcc-special-report-on-global-warming-of-1-5c-approved-by-governments/

Jeffers, Susan *Brother Eagle, Sister Sky: A Message from Chief Seattle* (Puffin Books, 1991)

Logan A. C., F. N. Jacka, and S. L. Prescott "Immune-Microbiota Interactions: Dysbiosis as a Global Health Issue," *Curr. Allergy Asthma Rep.* (2016) 16(2): 13 DOI: 10.1007/s11882-015-0590-5

Nisbet, E. K., J. M. Zelenski, and S. A. Murphy "The Nature Relatedness Scale: Linking Individuals' Connection with Nature to Environmental Concern and Behavior," *Environment and Behavior* (2009) 41(5): 715–40 DOI: 10.1177/0013916508318748

Reid, Chelsea A., Jeffrey D. Green, Tim Wildschut, and Constantine Sedikides "Scent-evoked nostalgia," *Memory* (2015) 23:2, 157–66 DOI: 10.1080/09658211.2013.876048

USDA *Soil Nuggets*, Fact Sheet (United States Department of Agriculture) www.nrcs.usda.gov/Internet/FSE_DOCUMENTS/stelprdb1101660.pdf

Wilson, Edward O. *Biophilia*, p. 10 (Harvard University Press, 1984)

Wilson, Edward O. *The Meaning of Human Existence*, p. 46 (Liveright Publishing/W.W. Norton & Co., 2014)

Cook's Notes

Standard level measuring spoon and cup measurements are used in all recipes.

Eggs should be large unless otherwise stated. The U.S. Food and Drug Administrations advises that eggs should not be consumed raw. This book contains dishes made with raw or lightly cooked eggs. It is prudent for more vulnerable people, such as pregnant and nursing mothers, people with weakened immune systems, the elderly, babies, and young children, to avoid uncooked or lightly cooked dishes made with eggs. Once prepared, these dishes should be kept refrigerated and used promptly.

For preference, use biodynamic or organic, locally sourced ingredients and opt for unwaxed citrus fruit.

Milk should be whole unless otherwise stated.

Fresh herbs should be used unless otherwise stated. If unavailable, use dried herbs instead but halve the stated quantities.

Garlic and onions are peeled unless otherwise stated.

Nuts. This book includes recipes made with nuts and nut derivatives. It is essential for those with known allergic reactions to nuts and nut derivatives and those who may be potentially vulnerable to these allergies, such as pregnant and nursing mothers, people with weakened immune systems, the elderly, babies, and young children, to avoid dishes made with nuts and nut oils. It is always prudent to check the labels of prepackaged ingredients for the possible inclusion of nut derivatives.

Pepper should be freshly ground black pepper and salt should be sea salt, unless otherwise stated.

Vegetarians should check the labels on cheese packaging to be sure it is made with vegetarian rennet.

Conversion Charts

Follow either U.S. standard measurements or metric measures; these units do not convert exactly.

Weight conversions

⅛ oz.	5 g		1 lb. 5 oz.	600 g
¼ oz.	10 g		1 lb. 7 oz.	650 g
½ oz.	15 g		1 lb. 9 oz.	700 g
1 oz.	25/30g		1 lb. 10 oz.	750 g
1¼ oz.	35 g		1 lb. 12 oz.	800 g
1½ oz.	40 g		1 lb. 14 oz.	850 g
1¾ oz.	50 g		2 lb.	900 g
2 oz.	55 g		2 lb. 2 oz.	950 g
2¼ oz.	60 g		2 lb. 4 oz.	1 kg
2½ oz.	70 g		2 lb. 12 oz.	1.25 kg
3 oz.	85 g		3 lb.	1.3 kg
3¼ oz.	90 g		3 lb. 5 oz.	1.5 kg
3½ oz.	100 g		3 lb. 8 oz.	1.6 kg
4 oz.	115 g		4 lb.	1.8 kg
4½ oz.	125 g		4 lb. 8 oz.	2 kg
5 oz.	140 g		5 lb.	2.25 kg
5½ oz.	150 g		5 lb. 8 oz.	2.5 kg
6 oz.	175 g		6 lb.	2.7 kg
7 oz.	200 g		6 lb. 8 oz.	3 kg
8 oz.	225 g			
9 oz.	250 g			
9¾ oz.	275 g			
10 oz.	280 g			
10½ oz.	300 g			
11½ oz.	325 g			
12 oz.	350 g			
13 oz.	375 g			
14 oz.	400 g			
15 oz.	425 g			
1 lb.	450 g			
1 lb. 2 oz.	500 g			
1 lb. 4 oz.	550 g			

Volume conversions

¼ teaspoon	1.25 ml		1½ cups/ 12 fl. oz.	350 ml
½ teaspoon	2.5 ml		1¾ cups/ 14 fl. oz.	415 ml
1 teaspoon	5 ml		15 fl. oz.	440 ml
2 teaspoons	10 ml		2 cups/ 1 pint/ 16 fl. oz.	475 ml
1 tablespoon/ 3 teaspoons/ ½ fl. oz.	15 ml		2¼ cups/ 18 fl. oz.	530 ml
2 tablespoons/ 1 fl. oz.	30 ml		2½ cups/ 20 fl. oz.	590 ml
3 tablespoons	45 ml		3 cups/ 24 fl. oz.	710 ml
4 tablespoons/ ¼ cup/2 fl. oz.	60 ml		3 cups plus 3 tablespoons/ 25⅓ fl. oz.	750 ml
5 tablespoons/ 2½ fl. oz.	75 ml		3½ cups/ 28 fl. oz	830 ml
5 tablespoons plus 1 teaspoon/ ⅓ cup/ 2¾ fl. oz.	80 ml		4 cups/ 1 quart/ 32 fl. oz.	950 ml
6 tablespoons	90 ml		4¼ cups/ 34 fl. oz.	1 liter
3½ fl. oz.	100 ml		5 cups/ 40 fl. oz.	1.2 liters
½ cup/4 fl. oz.	120 ml		6 cups/ 48 fl. oz.	1.4 liters
⅔ cup/5 fl. oz.	150 ml			
¾ cup/6 fl. oz.	175 ml			
¾ cup plus 1½ tablespoons/ 6¾ fl. oz.	200 ml			
¾ cup plus 2 tablespoons/ 7 fl. oz.	210 ml			
1 cup/ 8 fl. oz.	240 ml			
1 cup plus 2 tablespoons/ 9 fl. oz.	265 ml			
1¼ cups/ 10 fl. oz.	300 ml			

Conversion Charts

Linear conversions

¹⁄₁₆ inch	2 mm		10½ inches	26 cm
⅛ inch	3 mm		10¾ inches	27 cm
¼ inch	5 mm		11 inches	28 cm
⅜ inch	8 mm		11½ inches	29 cm
½ inch	10 mm / 1 cm		12 inches	30 cm
⅝ inch	15 mm		12½ inches	31 cm
¾ inch	2 cm		13 inches	33 cm
1 inch	2.5 cm		13½ inches	34 cm
1¼ inches	3 cm		14 inches	35 cm
1½ inches	4 cm		14½ inches	37 cm
1¾ inches	4.5 cm		15 inches	38 cm
2 inches	5 cm		15½ inches	39 cm
2¼ inches	5.5 cm		16 inches	40 cm
2½ inches	6 cm		16½ inches	42 cm
2¾ inches	7 cm		17 inches	43 cm
3¼ inches	8 cm		17½ inches	44 cm
3½ inches	9 cm		18 inches	46 cm
3¾ inches	9.5 cm		19 inches	48 cm
4 inches	10 cm		20 inches	50 cm
4¼ inches	11 cm			
4½ inches	12 cm			
5 inches	13 cm			
5½ inches	14 cm			
6 inches	15 cm			
6¼ inches	16 cm			
6½ inches	17 cm			
7 inches	18 cm			
7½ inches	19 cm			
8 inches	20 cm			
8½ inches	22 cm			
9 inches	23 cm			
9½ inches	24 cm			
10 inches	25 cm			

Oven Temperatures

All ovens vary and the times and temperatures given in the recipes should be used as a guide. Use your judgment to check when something is cooked. Ovens should always be preheated to the specified temperature.

Fahrenheit	Centigrade	Oven level
225°F	110°C	Warming food
250°F	120°C	Very low
275°F	140°C	Very low
300°F	150°C	Low
325°F	160°C	Low
350°F	180°C	Moderate
375°F	190°C	Moderate
400°F	200°C	Hot
425°F	220°C	Hot
450°F	230°C	Very hot
475°F	240°C	Very hot

Index

Index

L

Labneh 22
lean season ritual 83
leeks
    Leek and carrot coconut
    soup 117
    Leek and hazelnut risotto 123
legumes *see* dried beans
    lemons
    Oven-baked preserved lemon
    potatoes 42
    Preserved lemon spaghetti 41
    Preserved lemons 38–39
    Pucker-up preserved lemon
    salad 43
lentils
    Rhubarb and lentil curry 128
Lima bean and rosemary hummus
29
Lincoln, Abraham 147
Living Planet Index 82
love of food ritual 48
Luther, Martin 45

M

maple syrup 154
    Maple butter 156
    Maple-drizzled roast butternut squash
    32
    Maple-roasted carrots 154
Marinara sauce 97
Mars (god) 122
milk
    Peanut milk 86
mint 118
    Mint and cilantro chutney 118
    Rhubarb and mint sodas 142
    Spring pea, mint, and feta frittata 120
molasses
    Apple molasses 171
    Apple molasses and goat cheese
    pancakes 173
    Apple molasses gingerbread
    cookies 174
monocrops 18, 82, 87, 114, 128

muesli
    Strawberry chip muesli 73
mushrooms 148
    Mushroom, zucchini, and pumpkin seed
    canapés 148
    Savory spinach and mushroom
    porridge 94
mustard
    Cannellini beans, ale, mustard, and
    truffle stew 124

N

nature relatedness 8–9
    nature-related practice, developing
    a 19
New Potato salad 129
New Year 120, 123
    nature's new year ritual 115
noodles
    Green pea guac and wasabi soba 51
    Veggie stir-fry with peanut butter
    sauce 88
nuts
    Basil and Brazil nut pesto 85
    Cilantro and hazelnut pesto 85
    Leek and hazelnut risotto 123
    Parsley and walnut pesto 84
    Peanut butter 86
    Peanut milk 86
    Pine nuts 84
    Roasted beet and pistachio
    dip 53
    Veggie stir-fry with peanut butter
    sauce 88
    Zero-waste peanut pulp crackers
    87

O

Oatmeal honey bread 93
oats
    Oatmeal honey bread 93
    Savory spinach and mushroom
    porridge 94
Oneida 72

onions
    German onion pie 95
    Stone soup 110
onion skins
    Zero-waste veggie broth box 108
Orange-roasted cauliflower with dates 34
organic ingredients 18
Oven-baked preserved lemon potatoes
    42
Oven-roasted Brussels sprouts 153

P

Pancakes, apple molasses, and goat
    cheese pancakes 173
Parsley and walnut pesto 84
pasta
    Preserved lemon spaghetti 41
    Veggie stir-fry with peanut butter
    sauce 88
peanuts 87
    Peanut butter 86
    Peanut milk 86
    shells, recycling 86
    Veggie stir-fry with peanut butter
    sauce 88
    Zero-waste peanut pulp crackers 87
peas
    Green pea guac and wasabi soba 51
    Green pea guacamole 50
    Peas in a pod salad 67
    Spring pea, mint, and feta frittata 120
peelings and skins
    Zero-waste carrot powder 155
    Zero-waste tomato powder 57
    Zero-waste veggie broth box 108
pesto
    Basil and Brazil nut pesto 85
    Cilantro and hazelnut pesto 85
    Parsley and walnut pesto 84
pickles
    Deli-style dill pickles 134–35
    Pickled pumpkin 164
    Savory pickled plum and kale
    salad 71

Index

About the Author

The Mindful Kitchen was founded in 2016 by New York State native Heather Thomas, who now lives in Copenhagen, Denmark. Heather's MBA thesis at Copenhagen Business School on the business of food waste led her to open an eco-friendly eatery in the city's popular Vesterbro district. She soon discovered that what guests were *really* hungry for was help and advice on learning how to adopt more eco-friendly habits. In response, she developed The Mindful Kitchen, which offers people a path to greater well-being for both people and the planet by building a nature-related practice.

To spread the process of how to connect to nature with every bite, Heather has worked with eco-chef Tom Hunt, Havana Club, Sustain (a UK-based alliance for better food and farming), and with the Eden Project in Cornwall, UK. She has also trained in climate-change communications with Al Gore and the Climate Reality Project he founded.

Acknowledgments

Gratitude to the maple tree outside my window, which anchors me in the season; to the noisy seagulls that alert me to the passing of a workday; and to the brash magpie and the delicate songbird whose daily visits lift me out of myself.

Gratitude to the people in publishing who believed that I could write a book and made it better. To David Breuer for a bright idea; to Monica Perdoni for shaping it; to Stephanie Evans for finessing it; and to all the other talented individuals at Quarto.

Gratitude to everyone who instilled within me a love for the forces and the creatures that make food grow. To my Dad and departed Mom, who made harvest festivals highlights of our year. To my Auntie Lynn and departed Auntie Sig, for teaching me that the courage of my convictions was my most attractive feature.

The Mindful Kitchen will continue to grow to help people adopt a nature-relatedness practice for personal and planetary well-being. Gratitude to all those who have supported the vision, including: Torben and Mette Hedelund Thomasen, Kathy Oldridge, Sarah Snoxall, Anna Lippert, Maja Trolle, Pablo Flack, the indefatigable David Field, and the irrepressible Marian Reed.

Gratitude to the humans who make vulnerability feel safe; Jenny Jen, Jason, Neto, the Schu, Sus, and Ms. Zimmer. My German family for accepting me, warts and all. And to Tim Hohm. Such a small name, for such a person. Every day you teach me a little more about the grace of patience, humility, and quiet. It is a privilege to love you all.

Publisher's credits

The publisher wishes to thank Summerly Devito, Markus Kustermann, Sally Domingo-Jones, Stephanie Evans, and their families, for kindly allowing access to their homes during the photoshoots, and Stefan Barnes, Elise Gaignet, Lawrence Goozee, Niamh Jones, Tam, Elodie and Xavi Kustermann, George Miles, Chloe Murphy, Monica Perdoni, and Florence Trace for appearing in the photographs.

All photography by Xavier D. Buendia except for the images on the following pages from Shutterstock, Inc.:

© Shutterstock/Annaev 32; /kenary820 42; /zeeking 55; /foodonwhite 57; /Tim UR 72; /CWIS 78; /NewFabrika 79; George3973 87; /Jiri Hera 94; /Jiang Hongyan 106; /domnitsky 117; /Maks Narodenko 118, 150 ; /Valentina Proskurina 142; /Valentina Razumova 154; /lovelyday12 170; /garsya 164; and /Erickson Stock 176